Teamwork is vital for organisational success; it is also challenging and unsettling. This self-help guide is an invaluable resource for anyone managing and joining a team and provides practical exercises to remove any 'elephants in the room'.

Stephen Bach, Executive Dean, King's Business School, King's College London (KCL)

At last – a team effectiveness book written *by* practitioners *for* practitioners. I will return to it again and again.

Roger Minton, Head of Leadership Development, Anglo American

A pragmatic set of tools tried and tested by expert team coaches that brings some of the best thinking together in one place for team leaders and their teams. I love it.

Inge Maes, Chief People Officer, Sandoz

With the increasing prevalence of team-based work, understanding the psychology behind what enables high team performance is essential for all leaders. There is no 'magic bullet' to high team performance – it takes deliberate effort and so much more than team building! This book is highly accessible, filled with practical ideas and tips to be applied and tested in building a team that works together to achieve a common purpose.

Geraldine Percival, Group Head of Talent & Development, Asahi

Increasingly every team leader needs to be able to coach their own team so that it can function at more than the sum of its parts. Declan Woods is one of the most ex-perienced team coaches and from his work and research he provides 40 great team coaching tools and methods with very clear outlines that team leaders can use to coach their own teams.

Peter Hawkins, Professor, GTCI

THE
TRIUMPHANT
TEAM

40 dynamic practices to transform any team

DECLAN WOODS

The Triumphant Team
ISBN 978-1-739148-30-0
eISBN 978-1-739148-31-7

Published in 2022 by Teamgenie Books

A CIP record of this book is available from the British Library.

Contents

This book is dedicated to my wife Jo, who has made all this possible, with love

Foreword

'Teamwork', 'collaboration', 'pulling together' or however you choose to describe them are not fashionable corporate buzzwords; they are absolute fundamentals for successful teams that are becoming more and more essential, in our rapidly changing world.

Making sense of what creates a highly effective and ultimately high-performing team can be a head-scratching challenge in itself, let alone knowing where to start motivating a team to enact the required collective change, with or without the support of a practitioner team coach.

In creating *The Triumphant Team*, Dr Declan Woods brings together his wealth of experience as a top team, C-suite coach; his real life, hands-on executive business background; and his hugely credible psychological expertise to deeply support a team's ability to empower themselves to become their own coach, actively raising collective their self-awareness, and using powerful, transformative self-help techniques.

Research paints a clear and ever-building picture that teams who actively choose to invest time to focus on themselves become much more effective, through building shared clarity on the direction of the team, and have sharper goal orientation, more effective use of energies and resources and hugely improved internal and external relationships. This increased performance also feeds increased team member engagement at both a team and organisational level.

The Triumphant Team skilfully guides teams through fascinating theory and helpful models and processes that shine a light on old habits that need to be left behind, and new habits to be formed, powering forward team and organisational performance and ultimately meeting the challenges of a complex and fast-paced working environment, head on.

In my role, I see first hand the power of team coaching and supporting teams to unlock latent potential and reach new levels of performance, and the insights, tools and motivation that *The Triumphant Team* provides are a powerful ally to any team wanting to start this journey.

Andy Duncan, Head of Team Effectiveness, National Westminster Bank plc (Natwest)

Introduction

Great things in business are never done by one person.
They're done by a team of people.

Steve Jobs, American business magnate, industrial designer and investor

I chose this opening quote by the late Apple co-founder Steve Jobs, because it shows the power and potential of teams to achieve 'great things' and sets the tone for this book.

Now is the time for teams! The past few years have seen an increasing emphasis on teams in organisations. This is not surprising since they are the mainstay of corporations, government bodies, public sector entities and charitable institutions, and, as a growing body of research is confirming, one of the most effective interventions for improving organisational effectiveness and performance.

Why a self-help book for teams?

Working together as a team can be as challenging for its members as the many technical issues they face (if not more so), as Esther Derby and Diana Larsen found when researching what makes a great software development team. Teams are often ill-equipped to work through these challenges by themselves: I know this from first-hand experience, having received increasing numbers of calls asking for help. In my experience of working with teams globally, they find it difficult to be precise about what makes them effective, and harder still to know what to do when they are not.

I recognised these challenges, having been a member of or led teams for more than 30 years. This experience has spanned specialist in-house operational delivery and policy teams in the public sector, time-bound 'Big Four' consultancy project teams leading organisation-wide change programmes, leading huge 'teams of teams' as an army officer, and the leadership of whole functions in larger international corporate organisations. I have held both executive and non-executive director roles, and later consulted, coached and advised global teams for years.

Given these diverse and hard-won experiences, I thought I knew about teams – yet I have often struggled to understand them. They have been the source of both joy and frustration (and significant confusion), and I wasn't alone in my perplexity. I have received countless calls over the years from CEOs, chairs and human resources directors who were similarly baffled. In their descriptions of the team at hand, they generally described its members' interpersonal behaviours. Yet these were often symptomatic rather than causal factors of their teams' difficulties. Due to this lack of clarity about the contributory elements, team leaders either focused on the wrong things or ignored them: these did not achieve the desired effect.

I concluded that many team-level phenomena were slippery and hard to grasp, and that teams needed help to identify their fundamental drivers. Any team development work is in addition to its members' day jobs: they don't have the capacity to try to improve everything, and certainly not at the same time. But some things make a difference, while others do not. Teams needed a way of prioritising the 'must do' actions from the 'nice to do' ones.

To try to make more sense of teams and find a way of responding to these needs, I conducted postgraduate research studies at INSEAD business school in France and the University of Leicester in the UK, where I dived deeper into the psychology of teams and the drivers of team effectiveness. Based on four years of research and analysis, I created teamSalient, an online diagnostic tool to help teams discover how effective they are, and prioritise the actions for them to become great. This dramatically improved teams' self-insights, but I still believed they could take things even further.

teamSalient pointed a team to what it needed to focus on to improve, but it didn't go far enough to help teams put these insights into action. I created teamGenie, a specialist team coaching company, to help them tackle this challenge. To that end, over several years, I created and/or developed and field-tested the numerous techniques now contained in this book.

Who is this book for?

This book is for teams at work: whole teams, individual team members and team leaders. It also can be used by those tasked with supporting teams, whether internal to the organisation (e.g. human resources business partners or organisational development professionals) or external team practitioners (e.g. team coaches or consultants).

Team practitioners may be interested in the more technical material included in the Appendix.

Why should organisations focus on teams?

As recent research, reports and books show, there are numerous reasons why it makes sense for organisations to focus on teams, such as:

→ Raising productivity, building quality, reducing errors, improving patient safety and increasing innovative practices (see David Webster in *Creating Adaptable Teams*).
→ Strengthening a sense of identity and belonging to a team to improve wellbeing – both important factors in the more recent shifts towards virtual and hybrid working (see the Chartered Institute of Personnel and Development (CIPD) 2020 report, *Embedding New Ways of Working Post-pandemic*).
→ Improving personnel issues, such as reducing labour turnover and absenteeism (see Daniel Levi's book *Group Dynamics for Teams*).
→ Delivering organisational performance (see Sharma, Roychowdhury and Verma's journal of soft skills, entitled *Why Do Wilfully Designed Teams Fail?*).

In sum, organisations function on teamwork, and teams are vital to their success. Interested readers can find out more in the Further Reading and Resources section at the end of this book.

How to get the most from this book

This book contains a set of practices to help you build more effective teams. As a practical guidebook, it will help you understand and try out the practices quickly, and benefit from them. It's structured around six stages of team development – Orientating, Resolving, Collaborating, Achieving, Excelling and Re-orientating – contains 40 team practices, and is designed for you to dip in and out of the most useful parts, rather than to be read cover-to-cover.

Chapter 1 provides useful background on teams and the six stages of team development that I have identified. It answers questions such as:

→ What is a team?
→ What is an effective team?
→ How do teams develop?

Then, before setting out the practices themselves, it describes what a practice is and how teams can use them. Each practice is structured in the same way:

→ What this practice can help with – describes the issue or opportunity a team is facing.
→ About this practice – describes the practice and how it relates to the problem or prospect.
→ Time – the length of time it takes for a team to try the practice.
→ What you will need – sets out the materials and resources to carry out the practice.
→ Step-by-step guide – a sequence of steps to conduct the practice.
→ Top tips – to help you run the practice smoothly, avoid common pitfalls and make the most from it.
→ Variations – show alternatives to the main practice (NB: not all practices have variations included).

If you're looking for a heavyweight academic textbook on teams, this is not the book for you. A plethora of material about teams, their effectiveness and tools is available on the Internet and elsewhere. This book is practice-focused, but I have included authors' names to enable teams to find further resources and support for the practices themselves. (Fuller references are given with page numbers in the book or article where you will find what I have mentioned, and full details of the books and articles referenced are in the Further Reading section.)

In this book, the use of the word 'practices' is deliberate. I hope that you do just that: practise with them: try them, play with them, adapt them and make them your own. Enjoy them. I hope you find some of them useful, and that they improve the effectiveness of your own team or a team you are supporting.

In the spirit of improvement, I'm interested in what worked well for you, as well as where the practices might be even better. Do let me know how you find applying them, and how your team benefits from using them. Contact me at: declan.woods@teamgenie.com

Good luck!
Dr Declan Woods
CEO, teamGenie and teamSalient creator
www.teamgenie.com • www.teamsalient.com
Surrey, England, October 2022

Part I
Getting started with developing your team

Chapter 1
The six stages of team development

A whole is greater than the sum of its parts.

To misquote Aristotle, Greek philosopher and polymath

This classic quote shows the possibilities of teams: that their members can achieve much more together than by themselves. It underlines the potential of teams, and sets the stage for their development.

What is a team?

Definitions of 'team' abound. While there are lots of variations, there does seem to be agreement on certain elements. I define a team as:

> A collaboration between a recognised group of people drawing on individual capabilities and strengths, who are committed to working together interdependently to achieve a common purpose, and collective performance and learning goals.

(More details of this technical definition are included in the Appendix.)

Put simply, a team needs its members to work together towards some collective output that they couldn't achieve through the efforts of individuals working alone. Just because a group of people are called a team, it doesn't mean they *are* a team: they may be a group of people with little or no connecting purpose. However, team psychologist David Webster cautions us against the binary notion of 'Team/No Team' and suggests two more useful questions instead:

→ What is the work that the team is trying to accomplish together?
→ Where and how do team members need to work together to achieve that?

The answer leads us to a simple (but not always easy to admit) conclusion: if the work doesn't require people to operate together towards a common goal, there is no need for a team. Any efforts to try to create one artificially are unlikely to be successful.

If this is the case, save your time and energy. Some work is just best left to individuals, not teams.

What is an effective team?

There are numerous models of what constitutes an effective team. You may know of one already, or your organisation may have one in place. If so, use that. If not, then you might like to use the model of team effectiveness set out below, which forms the basis of teamGenie's proprietary team diagnostic tool, teamSalient (see www.teamsalient.com).

As discussed in the Introduction, teams are a key contributor to organisational performance. We also know that effective teams perform better. In *The Team Discovered: Dialogic Team Coaching*,

American team consultant Bennett Bratt explains this simply as 'how effective they are together drives their internal experience and their external impact' (p. 95). Practices help teams improve how they work together, so they become more effective and increase organisational performance.

As discussed earlier, my model of team effectiveness is based on years of quantitative and field research with teams, and consists of 16 'drivers' that together make a team effective (Table 1). These drivers are divided into three 'domains': 'Fundamentals', 'Facilitators' and 'Fire-ups', which stand for foundational, enabling and more individually focused areas respectively. They are described below and formed into a practice to evaluate your team's effectiveness in the Re-orientating stage (see Practice 37: 'Evaluating your team's effectiveness' on page 114).

Table 1: The 16 drivers of an effective team

No.	Driver	Driver description
Fundamentals domain		
1	Leadership	How leadership is provided within the team
2	Purpose	The reason the team exists and its contribution to the organisation
3	Team composition	Team membership and the skills of team members
4	Psychological safety	A shared belief that it is safe for team members to take risks and be themselves
5	Team glue	The strength of team member interdependence and cohesion
Facilitators domain		
6	Task processes	The steps a team takes to achieve its tasks
7	Communications	How a team exchanges information through conversations
8	Collaboration	How team members work together and with other teams
9	Conflict	Disagreements between team members based on a clash of interests or beliefs
10	Resources	Resources and development available to help the team carry out its work
11	Learning	How the team uses and develops its members' skills and improves from feedback
Fire-ups domain		
12	Achieves results	The team's results orientation and motivation to succeed
13	Self-management	How team members moderate their behaviour towards each other in the interests of the team
14	Courage	The strength to do the right thing for the team
15	Adaptability	The ability to adapt the team's thinking and behaviour, and respond at pace
16	Creativity	A culture of creating radically different ways of meeting stakeholder needs

The six-stage model of team development

Like people, teams develop over time. You may be familiar with the now classic 'Forming, storming, norming, performing' (FSNP) model created by Bruce Tuckman (1965) (if not, further notes on this are included in the Appendix). It describes the different stages that teams progress through from formation to maturity, as they evolve from starting out to working together effectively.

The model makes intuitive sense to many teams, and has entered the everyday lexicon of teams at work. Given this, I have used the FSNP model as the basis for showing a team's development journey, but updated it to reflect how teams operate in organisations today (Figure 1).

Figure 1: teamSalient's six stages of team development

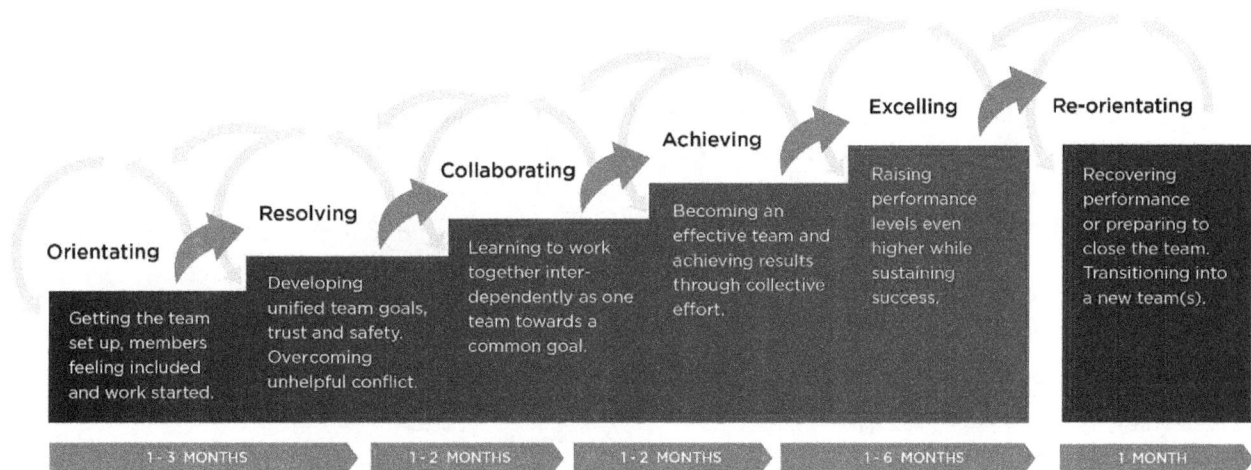

You will see that I use more aspirational language than Tuckman, replacing 'Storming' with 'Resolving', for example. The term 'Orientating' is intended to describe team members' orientation to each other, as well as towards new work.

While most teams 'Achieve' to some degree, few truly excel. So, I created a new stage – 'Excelling' – to raise the level of ambition for teams beyond performing satisfactorily. When teams do perform well, they often attract more work, and sometimes new team members and resources as a result. This wasn't reflected in Tuckman's original work, and so was added to this model. Similarly, teams don't simply disband (unless their work is completed). There is often a period of turnaround beforehand, so the 'Re-orientating' stage reflects both possibilities.

Tuckman's FSNP model emphasised the stages. While the teamSalient model also sets out distinct stages, the emphasis instead is on the shifts between them and the work involved in enabling these shifts. It also stresses the roles that both the team leader and team as a whole play in making these shifts.

Typically, it takes six to seven months for a team to progress from starting out to becoming fully effective and high-performing – although it can be quicker if the team has high levels of contact time and works together intensively. The teamSalient model shows the timings for each stage clearly, to help educate teams that excellence is not achieved overnight: there is no magic wand to become high-performing; it takes deliberate and disciplined action over time. The practices lay out these actions.

Goals and challenges

Each stage of team development has its own unique set of challenges, and these can stop teams from progressing if they're not worked through fully. It's also worth remembering that teams don't always move forwards: sometimes they can get stuck or slip backwards in their stage of development. Many teams stop short of excelling and underperform, but the good news is that there are many actions they can take to move beyond this.

The teamSalient model helps teams both identify their stage of development for themselves, and understand the challenges associated with that stage. This recognition can go some way to helping them understand that challenges are a normal part of development, and lets them know what to expect. It also shows the developmental goals for each stage, and proposes practices to help them make headway.

Table 2 describes the different stages of a team's journey, and the developmental goals associated with each to be completed.

Table 2: teamSalient stages of team development model

No.	Stage	Description	Goals
1	Orientating	A newly-formed team readies itself to start work. It is recruiting and integrating new members while allocating roles and tasks. Many aspects of the team and its work are unclear at this stage.	To form and set up the team. To foster a sense of belonging and loyalty to the team. To make it safe enough for members to contribute and start work.
2	Resolving	Whereas in the previous stage team members wanted to fit in, in this stage they seek to become more independent.	To develop unified team goals, values and processes. To resolve team conflict.
3	Collaborating	Team goals are clearer, and communication is open and task-focused.	To negotiate team member roles, priorities and processes (e.g. decision making). To develop positive team member relations.

4	Achieving	The team is effective, productive and delivering results. Members are clear about the team's goals, and work interdependently to realise them. Having resolved earlier difficulties, the team can focus its energy and collective efforts on results. The quality and quantity of work evolve throughout this stage of development.	To continue to develop team effectiveness. To get the job done well. To make more informed decisions. To remain cohesive. To maintain focus on the outcomes and results of collective work.
5	Excelling	A team is highly effective and has been achieving excellent results for some time. The team finds ways of sustaining success in the present, and ensuring it in the future.	To raise performance to even higher levels. To find ways of sustaining success. To recruit and integrate additional team members without loss of performance.
6	Re-orientating	Even high-achieving teams lose momentum over time. Typically, around 18–24 months after being formed, group effectiveness wanes and performance drops. This is normal but can have a significant effect on the team and its organisational performance. It is time to rethink the team's purpose: what work should it achieve now, and how should it be carried out?	To update the team's purpose, members, roles, ways of working, processes and norms. To revitalise the team and help it recover from declining performance. To ready the team to close while completing outstanding work and sustaining performance. To help members find new teams and successfully transition into them.

Why leadership matters

Leadership is critical to a team's success, because leader and team effectiveness are intrinsically linked. There are certain things that the leader cannot delegate to the team, including:

→ determining the team's vision, purpose and goals
→ deciding its membership (who is and isn't a member) and how the team is designed
→ holding accountability for the team's overall effectiveness and performance.

Once leaders have set the 'ends' (vision and goals), the team can work on the 'means' (the methods to achieve the ends). While anyone (team leader or member) can propose and lead a team practice, it may require the designated team leader to set the team development goals and prioritise the most valuable one with which to begin.

Getting ready to put the stages into practice

Statistician George Box's (1976) aphorism that 'all models are wrong, but some are useful', could apply to teams. By their nature, teams are complex, so any means to explain them through a single model is unlikely to be wholly accurate.

I have tried to simplify this complexity by defining a team and setting out what makes an effective team through the 16 'drivers' making up the teamSalient. I hope this approach and model are useful for you. The next chapter will introduce you to how to approach the practices with your team, and find out if change for your team is a worthwhile objective right now.

Chapter 2
How the practices work

Give us the tools, and we'll finish the job.

Sir Winston Churchill, British politician, former Prime Minister of the
United Kingdom, and wartime leader

It's not enough to do your best. You must know what to do, and then do your best.

W. Edwards Deming, American statistician, engineer and management theorist

As the saying goes, 'You can't build a house without tools', and teams need tools too. They are provided here in the form of practices to help teams develop, improve and perform. I like this Deming quote because it not only reminds us about the performance potential of teams, but also about being intentional in what they practice. Working hard is not enough for a team: it's about being clear on what they are doing and why, and building the capabilities to do their best work.

The definitions and six-stage model in Chapter 1 have set out what to expect as your team develops, so you can prepare to meet the challenges, achieve the goals associated with each stage and progress successfully on to the next one. While your team's development journey may not be smooth (no team's ever is), if you put the practices in this book into action, you will become a more effective team – and higher performance should follow.

This chapter introduces the concept of practices, their definition in this context and how you can use them with your team. Assuming a team knows 'what to do' (to paraphrase Edwards Deming) and can do it, the aim is for teams to engage in deliberate and intentional practices that help them become more effective.

When they do, effective teams are set to deliver stand-out performances.

What is a practice?

I define a practice as: 'How a team develops an agreed approach to carrying out its work, which, when repeated regularly, becomes a team process' (a full technical definition is included in the Appendix). I call the effort that teams put into deliberate and intentional development 'practice work'.

What is the theory behind practices?

The practices are underpinned by sound theoretical foundations and built on solid practical frameworks, summarised in the following principles:

→ strengths-based
→ openness to new possibilities
→ focused on finding solutions
→ identifying and celebrating what's working
→ learning from experience
→ active experimentation
→ improving team effectiveness.

(These are explained further in the Appendix.) Practices are part-construction, part-alchemy and part-adaptation.

How do practices work?

We start with the premise that teams – even great ones – can always improve and be better. Practices help teams to get there, and one way of doing this is through experimenting.

Here's how practices work. A team carries out a work task (e.g. reaching a decision on a major topic), but is dissatisfied with its approach or the outcome (or both). Perhaps a different outcome was achieved than planned, or it may have taken too long or been reached at too high a cost:

1. The team chooses a practice to try, and carries it out with a work task (e.g. collaborating with another team).
2. The team reflects on its experience and identifies the learning from this.
3. The team adapts the practice and repeats it, noting improvements to team effectiveness.
4. The team integrates the learning, adopts the practice as part of its regular processes and routines, and continues to refine it over time.

This means that when a process becomes habitual, it becomes a team routine or 'norm' – the normal way it does things. This approach works because, as Derby and Larsen tell us in their book, *Agile Retrospectives: Making Good Teams Great* (2006), 'Since experiments [practices] and changes are chosen, not imposed from above, people are more invested in their success' (p. xvi).

I believe the best practices arise from teams' needs as they carry out their work. This is very different from set-piece activities or exercises, which are often fixed and decided in advance of a team intervention (e.g. an icebreaker such as: 'If this team were an animal, what type would it be?'), which commonly forms the basis of team training.

Practices place the focus on learning rather than training. The most important condition is to make it safe to learn.

Here are some other tips to make practices work:

→ Being dissatisfied with the outcome of a work task creates the conditions for a team to want to learn and improve.
→ I don't subscribe to the proverb 'practice makes perfect', but do agree with American football

coach, Vince Lombardi, that 'practice makes permanent'. The challenge with practices is to keep going with them long enough to make them stick and make a difference. Persevere.

→ Remember, the purpose of team practices is to help improve team effectiveness and performance – it's not about the practices per se. Keep the focus on improving, and check the team is benefiting.

→ Adapting versus adopting practices – don't copy the practices wholesale. Adapt them to your team's needs, situation and context. Make them your own.

→ Hold them lightly – they may not work (at least at first). Trying them may feel clunky. This is normal – stick with them!

→ 'Test and adjust' – evolve practices over time as the team improves.

→ Experiments involve risks – is it risk-free enough for a team to take the practices and try something new? Make it safe.

Finally, trying anything new can feel a little alien for a start. Trust the practices. They have been tried before, and work. Take a deep breath, and give them a go.

Choosing a practice

The practices have been designed to help teams take the guesswork out of what to do in response to a specific challenge. It was well known that teams go through different challenges as they mature (see e.g. the work of Bruce Tuckman 1965, and his later 1977 updates with Mary Ann Jensen). The teamSalient six-stage model of team development sets out a contemporary version of this team maturity model, and is based on current uses of teams in organisations. (Further details of these stages, teams' needs at these stages and the related practices are shown in Table 3 below.)

The teamSalient model of team development is a deliberately directional one: it points them in the direction to become more effective and higher-performing. It is also directive, in that it sets out what teams can do (through practices) to improve. I know from experience that teams rarely follow this neat, linear route: the path towards team maturity and mastery can be an uneven one. Teams don't always progress – they can, and do, get stuck and experience inertia; sometimes they even regress and slip backwards.

In addition to picking a practice from the table, ask yourself, 'Will this practice help my team by…':

→ Preventing us from slipping backwards a stage? This is a minimum criterion for choosing a practice.

→ Getting unstuck and start to move us forwards? This is a useful start.

→ Progressing onto the next stage of development? This is the ideal state.

Before we reach the practices aligned to each of the stages of team development, there are three practices to start you off. These will help the team decide whether it's ready to go on the journey of developing. As Shakespeare's Prince Hamlet said, 'The readiness is all…'

Start with one or more of these practices to gauge the team's readiness.

Getting started with practices

There are numerous team practices on offer. Table 3 will help you choose which one best meets your team's needs. If you're not sure, just pick one and try it, and if it makes a difference, keep going with it and do more of it or repeat. If not, change the practice.

Table 3: The team practices by stage

STAGE DESCRIPTION	GOALS OF THIS STAGE	WHAT A TEAM NEEDS AT THIS STAGE	TEAM PRACTICES
The Orientating stage			
A newly formed team readies itself to start work. It is recruiting and integrating new members while allocating roles and tasks. Many aspects of the team and its work are unclear at this stage.	• To form and set up the team. • To foster a sense of belonging and loyalty to the team. • To make it safe enough for members to contribute and start work. • To connect team members to the team's purpose, bringing meaning and value to their work.	• Be clear about the team's purpose. • Understand team roles & responsibilities. • Understand team norms, processes and culture, etc. • Help members get to know each other. • To feel safe enough to start to trust the team leader and each other. • Develop a team identity to encourage membership. • Provide direction (vision) for the team.	Practice 4: Checking in and out with your team Practice 5: Getting to know each other Practice 6: Establishing ground rules to create psychological safety Practice 7: Identifying key team stake-holders Practice 8: Creating a compelling team vision Practice 9: Clarifying the team's shared purpose Practice 10: Establishing your team's goals Practice 11: Clarifying team member roles
The Resolving stage			
In the previous stage, team members wanted to fit in, in the 'resolving' stage, members seek to become more independent.	• Develop team goals, values, processes, and norms. • To resolve team conflict arising especially about role and task overlap(s) and the leader/leadership being offered. • To protect team members during disagreements. • To channel team members' energies towards tasks.	• Build (psychological) safety and trust. • Develop team goals, norms, and processes.	Practice 12: Improving dialogue in your team Practice 13: Creating a team working agreement Practice 14: Building trust between team members Practice 15: Tackling conflict Practice 16: Naming 'the elephants in the room' Practice 17: Helping your team build critical moment resilience

The Collaborating stage

Team goals are clearer, and communication is open, and task focused at this stage.	• To negotiate team member roles, priorities, and processes (e.g. decision making). • To develop positive team member relations.	• Develop levels of trust and relational strength between members. • Increase connections within, and between, teams. • Encourage collective ownership of tasks and more distributed/shared leadership. • Watch out for collaboration overload. • Work through conflicting priorities and competing resource allocation.	Practice 18: Forming a collaboration blueprint Practice 19: Creating a decision-making protocol Practice 20: 'Five-finger voting' decision making Practice 21: Identifying on-task, off-task, and anti-task behaviours in your team Practice 22: Generating creative ideas by 'brainwriting' Practice 23: Aligning your team

The Achieving stage

The team is effective, productive, and delivering results at this stage. Members are clear about the team's goals and work inter-dependently to realise them. Having resolved earlier challenges, the team focuses its energy and collective efforts on results. The quality and quantity of work evolves throughout this stage.	• To continue to develop team effectiveness. • To get the job done – well. • To make more informed decisions. To remain cohesive. • To maintain focus on the outcomes and results of collective work.	• Focus the team on high quantity and quality delivery of (outputs) work. • Seek, gather and provide feedback and monitor team performance. • Encourage information-sharing and collective decision-making. • Continue to improve team effectiveness.	Practice 24: Understanding stakeholder needs Practice 25: Increasing contributions in your team Practice 26: Improving your team's routines Practice 27: Conducting a pre-mortem to manage risks Practice 28: Learning in your team Practice 29: Playing the team joker

The Excelling stage

The team is highly effective and has been achieving excellent results for some time. The team also finds ways of sustaining success in the present and ensuring it in the future.	• To raise performance to even higher levels. • To find ways of sustaining success. • To recruit and integrate additional team members without loss of performance.	• Encourage a culture of learning, creativity and innovation to meet new and emerging needs. • Optimise team task processes. • Celebrate successes. • Engage with stakeholders about their changing needs.	Practice 30: Conducting a team debrief Practice 31: Identifying your team's rackets Practice 32: Getting into a creative flow Practice 33: Preventing your team from burning out Practice 34: Giving virtual gifts as acknowledgement Practice 35: Predicting your team's future

The Re-orientating stage

Even high achieving teams lose momentum over time. 18-24m after forming, group effectiveness wanes and performance drops. This is normal but can affect the team and its performance. At this point, it is time to rethink the team's purpose: what work should it achieve now, and how should it be carried out?	• To update the team's purpose, members, roles, ways of working, processes, and norms. • To revitalise the team and help it recover from declining performance. • On-board newly joined members to existing team norms and processes. or • To ready the team to close, while completing outstanding work and sustaining performance. • To help members find new teams and successfully transition into them.	• Help the team recover from setbacks – it's all in the recovery! • Renew the team's purpose, membership, processes, and practices as needs change. • Recognise achievements, celebrate successes. or • Support team members during change and transition or closure • Acknowledge and help the team accept loss/grieve.	Practice 36: Helping your team recover from setbacks Practice 37: Evaluating your team's effectiveness Practice 38: Coping with unexpected news and loss Practice 39: Improving your team's self-belief Practice 40: Planning for your team's closure

Chapter 3
Are you ready?

Let's start by gauging if your team is ready to begin its development. Two practices will help you decide that, and a third will help you ascertain if it's worthwhile.

Good luck!

Is your team ready for development now?

'Ready, steady, go!' or 'Ready, steady, no!'?

I use this phrase to explain to teams that embarking on a programme of development isn't necessarily the best course for every team or at that time. The conditions need to be optimal first to make the most of the opportunity.

This practice helps by identifying whether these conditions are in place: if not, it might be better to delay starting to develop the team until they are..

What this practice can help with

Teams are busy places. They may not yet be ready for, or committed to, the effort required to develop and improve. It can be useful for a team to establish this first to make best use of its time and resources.

About this practice

This evidence-based technique can be used by individual team members or the whole group to gauge your team's commitment to change. It also can help to explore any ambiguity between the costs and benefits of change for the team. This can be useful if, for example, the team leader is promoting change but the team is resisting it.

This practice works by your team listening to the words used by its members during conversations discussing potential changes. The language used reveals motives to change. It is a technique used in 'motivational Interviewing', developed by Stephen Miller and William Rollnick (2002) out of their frustrations in conversations about change that did not lead to it. The more 'change talk' used in a team, the more likely it is to change.

This is a quick practice which can give your team a rough indication of their motivation for change. It can be tried before a fuller assessment using Practice 2: 'Is your team still ready for development?', and at any point during team development if the team's motivation seems to have changed.

The practice uses the acronym DARN:

Desire – uses words such as 'want', 'wish' and 'like', which show that a team member wants something – a major factor in change. Examples to listen for are: 'I really want to do...', 'I would like to...'

Ability – team members must believe they can change for it to happen. Ability questions ask about what the team member can or could do without their committing to it. Examples of this 'change talk' could be: 'I would like to take on this new team role (desire), but I don't have the skills (ability).'

Reason – this reflects the need for a strong rationale. A team member may not yet want or feel capable of change, but they may be able to list the reasons for or against it. An example to listen for could be: 'I can see that it would be useful because...'

Need – this reflects the importance or urgency behind a change. Examples could be: 'I really need to...', 'I must...' or 'I've got to...'

Time

→ This practice is quick (5 minutes), and can be carried out by any team member.

→ Exploring change talk and resistance to change can take longer. Allow up to an hour for this.

What you will need

→ A short list of questions under the DARN headings.

→ A notebook and pen to record the language used in the conversation.

This practice can also work just as well virtually.

Step-by-step guide

1. This practice takes the form of a structured conversation between any number of team members. Anyone can lead it.

2. The person leading the conversation prepares and asks questions against the DARN headings, for example:

   → How much do we want this development/to develop? (Desire)

   → What resources do we need to be able to do this? (Ability)

   → Why do you think this development is needed? (Reason)

   → How urgent do you think the proposed project is? (Need)

3. Anyone in the team can look for the type of language being used by the team.

4. Team members can practise alternating between asking questions and listening to the answers until they can do both. Swap roles to build skills.

5. The overall question the team is answering is: 'Is the team ready now to develop?', with the possible answers being Yes/No/It depends.

6. The question of team readiness might depend on certain factors. The next question becomes: 'How do we create the conditions for successful team development?', with the team acting on the answer(s), followed by a third question:

7. 'Are there sufficient conditions to make a start and get going with the team's development now?'

8. Decide whether to start a development practice.

Tips for getting the most from this practice

→ Asking open-ended questions is one of the most effective ways to encourage change talk. Listen to the language used in the replies.

→ Don't create a monster – just ask a few questions to get the conversation started.

Is your team still ready for development?

Awareness is the greatest agent for change.

Eckhart Tolle, German spiritual teacher

Developing as a team is an 'opt-in' process. Teams can choose to engage in this, and to do so they need to be aware of what's involved – awareness is a precondition for change.

What this practice can help with

Before starting any practice, it can be useful to check the team is ready. The aim is to identify whether the conditions are in place for the team to gain the most benefit from a practice. The answers to this 'ready' question are seldom a straight 'Yes' or 'No', and are often 'It depends'.

This can lead teams to improve the conditions, much like a gardener preparing the soil before planting new seeds. For example, the team could be redesigned if it is too large to be effective.

About this practice

This practice could be led by a team leader or member, or conducted by members taking it in turns to ask questions. As the 'readiness' decision affects the whole team, it's important they work through these questions together. They will help the team decide if it's ready for the work involved in trying and applying the practices. If the conditions are not yet suitable, teams can decide whether to start their development and any corrective actions.

Time

→ A quick preliminary readiness assessment need only take 10 minutes.

→ A more thorough readiness check can take 30 minutes.

What you will need

Print out a copy of Table 4 below, and use it as a checklist and guide. This practice can also work just as well virtually, showing Table 4 on screen.

Step-by-step guide

1. This practice is carried out with the whole team working through the questions together.
2. Take each question in turn, and consider whether the team is ready or not. For example, a team that is 25 strong would most likely score a 'No' against the optimal size question. Where anything but a 'Yes' is scored, take time to consider what corrective actions would be needed to turn a 'No' or 'It depends' into a 'Yes', and list these in the far-right column.
3. Reach a clear agreement on the corrective actions to be taken as a team, who is responsible for them and the deadline to complete them.
4. Some of these actions could be carried out in parallel with the practices, and so don't need to delay things. Other, bigger actions (e.g. changes to the team) could take longer, and it might be best to delay the start of the practice until afterwards.
5. By looking at the consolidated actions required, assessment can be made as to where the priorities lie for corrective action, and to what extent these might impact the development programme (e.g. delay it or even make it untenable).
6. From the long list of actions at step 3, reach a clear agreement in the team on the priority collective actions.

Table 4: Team readiness indicator questionnaire

Source	Indicator question	Ready	Importance	Corrective action(s)
Leader/team/ organisation/all	E.g. Are we committed to being developed as a team?	Yes/No/ It depends on…	High/Medium/ Low	E.g. Discuss with team members individually, then together. Clarify what's involved. Check for commitment.
Team	Are we a team? Are team members reliant on one another to achieve collective results?		High	
Team	Is our team the optimal size for collective work? (5–9 members)		Medium	
Team	Is our team's membership likely to be sufficiently stable throughout the development?		Medium/Low	
Team	Are there obstacles that might hinder our team development?		Medium	
Team	How motivated are we towards being developed? Is change needed?		Medium/High	
Team member	Are individual team members performing? If not, do these need to be addressed first/separately?		Medium	
Leader	Is the team leader motivated for the team to be developed?		High	
Leader	Is the team leader open and willing to change personally?		High	
Organisation	Can the team gain the resources it needs from the organisation?		Medium	
All	Is the team clear on its purpose?		Low	
All	Is the team willing to devote the time needed to develop?		Low	
All	Is the team very 'unhealthy'? (Significantly dysfunctional)		High/Medium	
Overall team readiness (High/Medium/Low)?				**Priority collective actions:**

Source: adapted from Clutterbuck (2015)

Tips for getting the most from this practice

→ The most critical readiness indicators are ones involving the team leader and those marked as 'High' importance. If time pressed, start with these.

→ Recognise that the perfect conditions for team development rarely exist.

Variations

→ Reduce the number of questions by focusing on those that suggest your team is not yet ready.

→ If you are a team leader, you could conduct a preliminary readiness assessment yourself before proposing any team development, and take early action to address any areas needed.

Is the change worthwhile for your team?

The only person that likes changes is a baby with a wet nappy.

Bear Grylls, British adventurer, writer, television presenter and businessman

Not everyone welcomes change – including teams. They need to see the benefit in making changes, and this practice helps them do that.

To change or not to change, that is the question?

Adapted from *Hamlet*, 1603

This adapted, well-known Shakespearean quote reminds us that teams can choose whether to change, and that making it meaningful and worthwhile can help create a case for it.

What this practice can help with

Teams are busy places. For teams to engage in making meaningful changes, they must be worthwhile – big enough to make a difference, but not so big as to be impossible.

While this practice can be used by your team for any change it is considering, it's included here to help them decide if it wants to engage in some of the practices, and if everyone is committed to the efforts to make them work.

About this practice

This practice helps teams to establish whether a change is realistic and, if so, whether there is sufficient benefit from the change compared with the effort involved in changing.

Time

This can be a quick practice, and used alongside Practice 1: 'Is your team ready for development now?' (on page 16) for a rapid readiness assessment, or as part of a longer change planning process.

What you will need

Print out a copy of Table 5 (2 x 2 matrix) below. This practice can also work just as well virtually, showing Table 5 on screen.

Step-by-step guide

1. Use the 2 x 2 matrix to gauge if the change is:

   → Valuable – is the change useful and sufficiently important to the team and/or its stakeholders? Are the advantages attractive?

   → Achievability – is the change feasible, realistic and achievable?

2. As a team, ask and answer the following questions:

    → Is there sufficient difference between the current state and potential end state after this change to make it worthwhile?

    → Is there enough benefit to make it valuable?

    → What assumptions are we making about the benefits of change (or otherwise), and what testing of those assumptions can we do to ensure they are accurate or otherwise?

    → Does this team have the skills to make the change? What capabilities do we need? How will we get them (recruit, train, borrow, etc.)?

    → Is the change realistic and achievable within the timescales and current resources? If not, can the timescales and resources be (re)negotiated?

3. Based on the team's answers to these questions, decide whether you wish to undertake the team development.

Table 5: Team development value–achievability matrix

	Achievability		
Value	Mission impossible	Doable with some effort	Relatively straightforward
Big	Find workaround	Give it a go	Go for it
Average	Consider your options	Possibly	Worth it
Small	Don't bother	Probably not	When time permits

Source: Adapted from Tannenbaum and Salas (2021)

Tips for getting the most from this practice

You could stress-test Achievability by arguing the opposite – that the change is impossible. Is the change still then doable?

Variations

In the case that the team development appears not worth pursuing, consider alternative ways of delivering the value you seek, and run the same process against it.

Part II
Practices for the six stages

Chapter 4
The Orientating stage

A journey of a thousand miles begins with a single step.

Lao Tzu, ancient Chinese philosopher and writer

This book contains six stages of development for a team to progress through on its journey to becoming higher performing. While this takes some time, and may look a long way ahead, this quote reminds us that everything starts somewhere – and encourages teams to make a start.

The Orientating stage sees newly-formed teams ready themselves to start work. They are engaged in recruiting and integrating new members, and deciding and allocating roles and tasks to team members. Many aspects of the team and its work are unclear to its members at this stage. While this can be frustrating and anxiety-provoking for some, it is normal and reflects this early forming stage in the team's maturity.

If your team hasn't been designed yet, this can be carried out now. If it has, a team can be set up for success through a launch process (explained below).

Team goals at the Orientating stage

To progress in its development (and move on to the next stage, Resolving), your team will need to work through and achieve the following goals:

→ form and set up the team
→ foster a sense of belonging and loyalty to it
→ make it safe enough for members to contribute and start work
→ connect its members to the team's purpose, bringing meaning and value to their work
→ launch the team successfully

What teams need at the Orientating stage

This first stage of development presents teams with several challenges, including bringing different elements together, creating the foundations to be successful, and ensuring everyone sets off in the same direction.

The work to complete at this stage includes:

→ being clear about your team's purpose – why it exists, including from different stakeholder perspectives
→ clarifying the vision for the team, so everyone is moving in the same direction
→ understanding individual member roles and responsibilities, and how these roles work together
→ helping members to get to know each other

→ feeling safe enough to start to trust the team leader and each other in the team

→ developing a team identity, to encourage cohesion and increase a sense of belonging

→ understanding team norms, processes and culture – i.e. how the team gets work done

→ launching the team – getting under way.

Most of these areas provide clarity and certainty for team members, and start to make it safe to begin work. The team is then ready to launch.

The Orientating stage practices

Teams that have not been well designed and set up tend to underwhelm and underperform, and it needn't be this way. The purpose of practices at this stage is to lay the foundations for a newly-formed team to be successful: think of them like the foundations of a house, providing solid underpinnings on which the rest is built. Many aspects of team dysfunction can be traced back to how a team was set up in the first place – so it's well worth paying attention to this and the related practices for the Orientating stage.

Take, for example, the IT leadership team of a global consumer goods company I coached. The team consisted of 14 members, all with discrete roles and individual projects to deliver. This team was a little too large to operate efficiently (just trying to hear everyone's voice in a conversation took a long time), the members' roles were not aligned to allow them to work together interdependently and, given the disparate nature of their individual projects, they were not clear on the overall team purpose and why they needed to work together.

A piece of redesign work helped create more clarity and alignment, then enabled the team to launch well.

The practices for this stage will help your team to:

→ understand who its key sponsors and/or stakeholders are, and what they need from the team (Practice 7 on page 34)

→ clarify why it exists, and its purpose (Practice 9 on page 38)

→ understand its goals and the work it must do (Practice 10 on page 40).

Launching your team

The Orientating stage practices can be carried out separately, or combined into a series of linked sessions that together form a 'team launch'. Launches are not commonplace in teams, but they can be an incredibly valuable opportunity to bring together the work entailed in these separate practices into a cohesive whole before the team starts work (or even to relaunch the team if it hasn't got off to the best start).

Team launches are often held off-site (away from the normal place of work) to minimise distractions, and allow the team to focus on launching well. This can take one to two days. Time spent on these practices beforehand is well spent, and will save time later.

The outputs of these various launch activities can be written down in a one-page 'team charter': this synthesises a team's purpose and goals, etc. in one place – the process of creating and displaying all the important elements of a charter can be galvanising.

Use Table 6 to record the results of your team's practices and discussions.

Table 6: Team charter

Team purpose Why does the team exist?	**Common goals** What results do we want to deliver?	**Core values** What is most important to us as a team?
Team composition Who is on this team?	**Team member roles** Which roles are needed?	**Key stakeholder(s)** Who are the team's key stakeholders, and what do they need from us?
Working agreements How do we agree to work together? What are our ground rules?	**Decision making** How will we make decisions?	**Communications** How and what will we communicate to others outside the team?

Source: adapted from Woudstra (2021)

However, before a team embarks on these launch practices, there are others to undertake relating to the human needs of joining and belonging to a new team:

→ helping team members get to know each other (or better) (Practice 5 on page 30)
→ agreeing some basic ground rules to create psychological safety (Practice 6 on page 32).

This is both a busy and vital developmental stage: it's worth spending the time on the practices to set up the team for success.

Good luck!

Checking in and out with your team

We must slow down to a human tempo, and we'll begin to have time to listen.

Thomas Merton, American Trappist monk, writer and theologian

Keen to get under way, teams can rush and skip over important things, including helping their members get to know one another. In my experience, when teams invest the time, they regain it later.

What this practice can help with

Teams operate at pace with everyone focused on their 'own bit'. Members often arrive for meetings distracted by other things, whether work or non-work related. Most team meetings start with the question, 'How is everyone?' with everyone replying, 'Fine, thanks,' in a predictable social routine. This approach lacks human connection, and misses the opportunity for the team leader and members to understand what is going on for everyone in the team.

Check-in and check-out practices fill this gap, allowing members to settle into the team's work. Just as significantly, check-ins/outs allow a team to surface and understand any hidden undercurrents. Without check-ins, these 'beneath the surface' topics often remain out of sight, only tending to emerge later in a worse state.

This practice makes a difference: a study by Emmett Perry and colleagues at the University of Missouri with 26 teams found that those who spent the time before a project sharing personal experiences, outperformed those who started working straightaway.

About this practice

The purpose of checking in/out is to slow the pace sufficiently to allow your team's members to connect with one another, express what is important to them, and to be heard by others in the team.

Check-ins/outs are important to the Orientating stage because they help team members get to know and connect with each other and, through disclosure, foster psychological safety. Practically, check-ins also get everyone involved from the start of a team meeting. Otherwise, 'When someone doesn't speak at the beginning [of a meeting] ... that person has tacit permission to remain silent for the rest of the session,' argue agile coaches Esther Derby and Diana Larsen (p. 5).

This is one of the simplest practices in this book. When practised regularly, it marks the start of a team meeting by creating a different tone, and gets everyone contributing from the outset.

Time

→ This practice can be done in as little as 5 minutes.

→ Add more time for more people.

What you will need

No materials are necessary for this practice to keep the focus on team members. This practice can also work just as well virtually.

Step-by-step guide

1. Invite team members, one by one, to speak and say a few words about whatever is on their mind that is significant for them in that moment. This could be as simple as asking team members to talk about their hope for a team meeting. It's helpful to indicate the length of response sought, e.g.:

   → 'We're keen to hear what's going on for you, but as time is short, please try to be concise and limit yourself to a minute or two.'

   → 'Please say two words that sum up how things feel different for you after today's meeting.'

2. While one person is speaking, the rest of the team listens actively.

3. Choose how you will respond to acknowledge and address concerns. You could simply ask, 'What do you need?', or 'What help can the rest of the team provide?'.

4. Choose whether to go round the table, or suggest members speak in random order – either way, ensure no one is missed out.

5. It is acceptable for anyone (but hopefully not everyone) to say, 'I pass.' Saying 'I pass' still ensures every voice is heard while giving them the opportunity to speak.

Tips on getting the most from this practice

→ Checking in/out requires safety, practice and discipline. It can take teams a while to feel safe enough to check in more deeply. It's also easy for teams to slip back and engage with each other superficially. Make it safe, and stick with it.

→ Welcome whatever is said – sharing openly builds connection and trust in a team.

→ There can be a temptation for teams to get down to business straightaway, and skip checking in, but this is time well spent. Going more slowly initially allows teams to go faster later.

Variations

You could try checking in/out using picture cards to stimulate thought, for example:

→ spreading a pack of cards out on the floor, then asking each person to choose a card that echoes how they are feeling as they arrive

→ then in turn, inviting each to say a few words as to why they have chosen that card, and what meaning they are finding in the image.

Getting to know each other

I don't like that man. I must get to know him better.

Abraham Lincoln, lawyer, statesman and 16th President of the United States of America

It is human nature to be wary of people dissimilar to us, but our opinion of others can change when we get to know them – and this is a crucial activity for newly-created teams.

What this practice can help with

Newly-forming teams need to integrate members, and key to this is helping them get to know each other. Doing this early in the life of a team, or after changes in its membership, is an important part of fostering a sense of belonging and loyalty to the team, speeding up its formation.

About this practice

Three mini-practices are outlined below to help team members get to know each other – an important part of the Orientating stage of team development. They can be used in newly-formed teams, and to onboard new members into existing teams.

Time

The mini-practices below give the timings.

What you will need

The mini-practices below give the tools and resources. These can also work just as well virtually.

Step-by-step guide

Who's in the room?

This is a quick way of everyone introducing themselves, so that other team members know who's in the room. It takes just 5 minutes or so, and doesn't require any materials. Teams that know each other already can skip this practice and start with one of the others.

1. Invite each team member in turn to say hello, then introduce themselves against pre-agreed prompts (e.g. name, job role, little-known fact). For example, say: 'Tell us about yourself in one sentence or less/no more than five words.'
2. Continue until every team member has spoken.
3. The order can be sequential (one team member in turn in order of seating, to the left or right), by 'popcorn' (randomly) or 'baton passing' (with the last team member speaking deciding who should introduce themselves next). This ordering process also applies to the other practices.

My desert island

Many people will be familiar with this practice from the long-running BBC Radio 4 programme, *Desert Island Discs*: an invited guest is asked to pick eight pieces of music, a book and a luxury item to take with them if stranded on a desert island, and share them with listeners.

Here, we invite team members to say which items they would take on their desert island. Again, this is a quick practice.

1. Invite each team member in turn to introduce themselves, and say what three items they would take with them if stranded on a desert island.
2. (If time permits) Invite the rest of the team to ask any questions to deepen their understanding of the team member.

My personal object

This is a practice from work with family systems, and a more personal way of finding out about other team members. Each team member brings along and talks about an object that's meaningful to them: it should tell the rest of the team something that they might not otherwise know about each other.

Allow up to 5 minutes per team member to get the full benefit from this, although it can take longer.

1. Invite each team member in turn to show and/or describe their personal object.
2. Explain its significance to others, why they chose it and what it tells team members about them as part of a team.
3. (If time permits) Invite the rest of the team to ask any questions to deepen their understanding of the team member.

Tips on getting the most from this practice

→ Use these mini-practices by themselves, or one after the other.

→ Using them progressively helps build team psychological safety: it allows members to test reactions to what they have said before deciding whether to reveal more about themselves.

→ Team members will take their cue from the leader as to how much to reveal, so it helps if the leader goes first and is courageous about what they reveal.

→ Try to encourage meaningful disclosure.

→ Valuable, breakable or dangerous objects are best avoided being brought into work. Bring a photograph instead.

→ Recognise that objects can be deeply personal, so be sensitive when discussing them and ask any questions with care.

→ 'My personal object' works well when thought about in advance. Prime the team.

Variations

→ The 'On my desert island' practice can be as silly or serious as you like. You could omit practical items (e.g. a life raft) by saying that your basic survival needs are already met, and focus on light-hearted items (e.g. favourite drink) or vice versa.

→ If team members know each other already, personal objects could be pre-placed in the room, with members trying to guess who each object belongs to before the owner then claims their object.

Establishing ground rules to create psychological safety

Being able to show and employ oneself without fear of negative consequences of self-image, status or career.

William Kahn, Professor of Organisational Behaviour, Boston University

Although a popular concept, psychological safety and how to acquire it is still not clearly understood. This practice explains how and why we create ground rules, and how they create safety.

What this practice can help with

In answering 'What makes one of our teams effective?', Google's researchers, studying 180 teams, identified psychological safety as being the most important factor, says author Charles Duhigg in his 2016 *New York Times* article.

Harvard professor Amy Edmondson (1999), who popularised psychological safety, describes it as 'a shared belief held by members of a team that the team is safe for interpersonal risk-taking'. There is significant research confirming that it is essential to organisational performance. It's also vital if a team wants to change because all change involves risks and to take them, we need to feel safe to experiment with new ways of working.

About this practice

There is no single practice that creates psychological safety. It is formed and forged through a shared and ongoing set of experiences when teams work together. Teamwork behaviours can be agreed and worked on consciously, taking the form of agreeing basic ground rules.

When practised regularly, these behavioural 'rules' become team routines that help create psychological safety. This is important at the Orientating stage to make it safe enough for members to start working together. In this practice, your team discusses and agrees its ground rules to achieve this.

Time

→ This practice can be conducted in about 20 minutes.

→ Prime this practice by reflecting on how the team has worked together so far.

What you will need

Minimal to no materials are needed, although writing the ground rules on a flip chart, where your whole team can read them, can be useful. This practice can work virtually with some adaptations and showing Figure 2 (page 35) on screen.

Step-by-step guide

1. As a team, discuss and agree the ground rules that describe how your team would like to work together (see examples below) by asking the following questions:

    → How psychologically safe is it to speak up, hold a minority view or disagree in this team?

    → What do we need to agree to keep things safe between us?

    → What do we need to agree to promote learning?

    → What do we need to agree to keep things relevant and useful?

2. Check for understanding and clarity, e.g. ask: 'What does being open mean in *this* team?'
3. Invite everyone in the team to contribute, so they buy into these ground rules.
4. Check that they're all willing to agree to them.
5. Agree what will happen if the ground rules are broken (it will happen), and ask how team members wish to hold each other to account for breaches. (This is as much the team's responsibility as the leader's.)
6. Check progress and update the rules periodically to ensure they are current and reflect the latest team challenges.

Here are a few possible team ground rules:

→ Listen – to respect and understand.
→ Say what needs to be said – share your views, questions and curiosity.
→ Don't interrupt team members.
→ Speak for approximately equal time to others.
→ Respond fully when asked a question by a team colleague.
→ Use specific examples, and agree on what important words mean.
→ Be willing to influence and be influenced.
→ Focus on mutual team interests, not (fixed) individual positions.
→ Explain your intentions and reasoning.
→ Discuss undiscussable topics with the whole team.
→ Design next steps jointly as a team. (List adapted from Schwarz 2002.)

Tips on getting the most from this practice

→ Psychological safety is often considered something a team has or doesn't have, but it can be created and increased, or just as easily destroyed, through team members' behaviour.
→ That said, we cannot make teams completely safe and, as the classic study by psychologists Yerkes and Dodson showed back in 1908, an amount of anxiety is needed for teams to perform.
→ Like any agreement, ground rules can be broken. Writing them down can be a useful way of reminding team members what has been agreed.
→ As creating ground rules is a familiar activity, teams may want to skip or rush this practice. Instead, ask members to contribute rules that they have learned work well in other teams.

Variations

→ Count to 20. This time prevents careless reactions affecting safety.
→ Offering affirmations to team members fosters team safety, e.g. by saying 'thank you' or giving a gift virtually (see Practice 34 on p. 104).
→ Think about the best team you have worked in: what ground rules existed in that team could you adopt?
→ Think about the worst team you have worked in: you might still be able to learn valuable lessons from this experience. What ground rules, had they existed in this team, would have improved it?

Identifying key team stakeholders

O wad some Pow'r the giftie gie us/To see oursels as ithers see us!
[Oh, would some power the gift give us/To see ourselves as others see us!]

Robert Burns, lyricist and national poet of Scotland

This quote by Burns inspires us to increase our awareness, and nowhere is this more important for teams than understanding their key stakeholders better.

What this practice can help with

Teams are created for a reason: to meet the needs of key stakeholders. However, neither stakeholders nor their needs are always that obvious to a team, which can distort what a team focuses on and produces.

About this practice

There are many ways of understanding a team's stakeholders and their needs, including stakeholder mapping exercises, in-depth interviews and so on. We use the intelligence within a team to identify its key stakeholders, and a practice to start to understand what is important to them. The related stakeholder practice (Practice 24 on page 80) can be used to understand their needs more deeply. Identifying and understanding stakeholders' needs are important to this stage to inform the team's work and goals.

Time

→ Creating and discussing a stakeholder profile/persona can take 15–20 minutes.
→ Mapping and discussing stakeholders can take 20–60 minutes, depending on their number and needs' complexity.

What you will need

→ Flip charts and marker pens
→ Teams could enlarge and print copies of Figure 2 below to complete.

This practice can work virtually with some adaptations.

Step-by-step guide

1. Identify your main stakeholders by asking the following questions:

    → Who is the team accountable to – e.g. clients, regulator, the public?
    → Who are the key sponsors of this team?
    → Who else is dependent on this team?
    → Who will be impacted by our team's work?
    → Who else inside and outside the organisation does the team need to collaborate with?

2. As a team, ask:

    → Which stakeholder(s) can support this work? (Power)

→ Which stakeholder(s) can disrupt this work? (Influence)

3. Then, plot these stakeholders into Figure 2 according to the extent of their:

   → power – level of influence
   → interest – how much they will be affected by the team's work, and how engaged they are with it.

4. Agree actions in the team to manage the various stakeholder groups, paying particular attention to the high-power/high-interest group.

5. As a team ask, 'Which stakeholders need to be communicated/consulted with, and about what?'

6. Again, as a team and for each stakeholder group in turn, answer the following questions:

   → What does each of these stakeholder groups need from this team?
   → What are the different stakeholders' expectations, and what does the team need to do to deliver these?
   → Does our team's vision, purpose, goals and ways of working align with our stakeholders and key others?
   → How are our team and the wider context changing? What does this mean for our team's vision, purpose and goals? How can the team influence, as well as be influenced by, the context?
   → What does the future hold for our team in this changing context, and how can we respond to this?

7. Decide which team member will be responsible for engaging with and representing each stakeholder. Agree how they will go about this, and when.

Tips on getting the most from this practice

→ Get inputs from everyone in the team to ensure you have not missed important stakeholders. Check your list with others outside of the team.

→ There can be sensitivities about where your stakeholders appear in the 2 x 2 matrix. Take care who sees it!

→ Focus on the things that only your team can provide to each stakeholder.

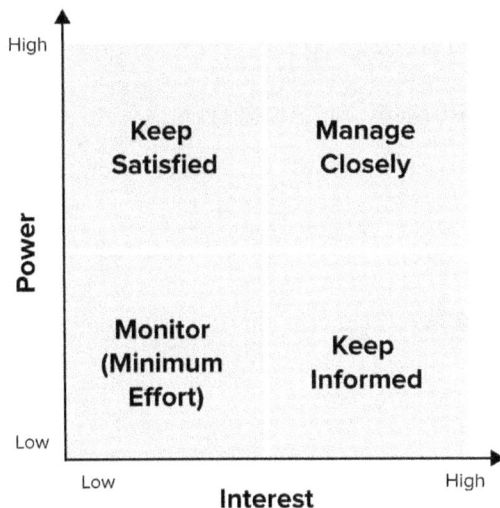

Figure 2: Stakeholder power–interest matrix

Source: https://www.mindtools.com/pages/article/newPPM_07.htm

Creating a compelling team vision

Our destiny is not written for us. It's written by us.

Barack Obama, 44th President of the United States of America

I love this quote by former President Obama because it reinforces that a team's future is in its own hands, and something teams can choose to engage with.

What this practice can help with

Teams need to know the direction they are taking to fulfil their purpose and engage members in their work. Creating a vision statement can meet this need.

About this practice

A vision can act as a guiding force for a team, and help explain its work. According to Canadian coaches who work with teams, Jacqueline Peters and Catherine Carr, it can 'provide a vivid, idealised future that inspires and energises people to achieve a greater purpose in their work' (p. 47).

This practice explains how teams can go about creating a vision for the *team*, which is different from creating a vision for the *organisation*. It's common for the team leader to decide the team's vision (the 'ends'), with the team establishing the 'means' by which they will do that. If the leader decides to engage the team in this, these practices can help. If not, these practices will aid the leader in this task.

This practice offers options for your team (or you as a team leader) to create a vision and check your team's alignment with it. These methods are adapted from the team visioning work of Peters and Carr, and a team alignment process by American team consultant Miles Kierson (2009). The 'storyboarding' practice is based on one by Dave Gray and colleagues in the book *Gamestorming* (pp. 71 and 87–89). Creating a compelling team vision is important to the Orientating stage because it starts your team moving in the same direction. These practices can be carried out as part of a team launch alongside other practices.

Time

This visioning practice can take 30 to 40+ minutes.

What you will need

Use visual materials to create the storyboard and newspaper headline (this practice can also work virtually with some adaptations):

→ Flip charts
→ Coloured pens
→ Sticky notes.

Step-by-step guide

Creating a vision statement through dialogue

Discuss the following questions, and agree answers as a team to create your vision:

→ What do we aspire to become as a team? What do we want to be?
→ What do we dream of as a team?
→ What do we want the future to hold for us?

→ What makes us unique and different from other teams?

→ What is being asked of us as a team?

→ What can we offer in return?

Creating a team vision statement through storyboarding

The aim of this activity is to tell a motivational story: the ideal future for this team:

1. Split the team into subgroups, each telling their own story before combining them.
2. Task the subgroup to narrate the story to the rest of the group.
3. Taking 20–25 minutes, agree an ideal future for the team.
4. Determine what steps the team needs to take to get there.
5. Draw each step as a sequence of large images or scenes in newspaper format. Include:

   → Cover – the big success story; what results have been achieved?

   → Headlines – the substance of the cover story; what has been the team's impact?

   → Sidebars – reveal interesting facets; what is it like to work in the team?

   → Quotes – from anyone related to the story; what are team members saying?

   → 'Brainstorm' – initial ideas for the cover story

   → Images – to support the written content with illustrations.

6. Each subgroup now tells their story of 'the ideal future for this team'.
7. Seek feedback from the rest of the team: what has inspired them about the story they heard? What themes emerged? What new observations, insights, 'aha!' moments did they gain?
1. Combine the different subgroup stories into a single team story.
2. Agree actions.

Tips on getting the most from this practice

→ Vision statements create a mental image of the team's goals. Make them visual and memorable to inspire actions. Is your vision clear and compelling to the team and stakeholders?

→ A team's vision is different from its organisation's. Check that they align.

→ To guide medium to longer-term team activities, a vision should be enduring, forward-focused and not readily achievable. Is yours? Does it excite and motivate the team?

→ A team may have a vision but not be committed to it. Checking this can be as important as creating it.

→ Check the team's progress towards realising it periodically. Refresh the vision if needed.

Variations

This practice is like the one above, but instead uses a newspaper headline approach to create a team vision. Follow the steps above, but rather than working on a storyline, draw the front page headline of a popular newspaper that describes the situation *after* the team's vision has been achieved.

Clarifying the team's shared purpose

Purpose affirms trust, trust affirms purpose, and together they forge individuals into a working team.

General Stanley McChrystal, United States Army (retired)

This quote from former US General McChrystal explains the vital importance of purpose when forming a team.

What this practice can help with

Teams are not always clear about the reasons for their existence, particularly if they have existed for some time and the original members have left. A key task for teams at this stage is to get ready to start their work.

Clarifying a team's shared purpose provides useful context for the team, helps bring meaning and value to its members' work and unites individual contributions. There is strong research evidence on the benefits of purpose work (e.g. see the 2018 article by Michigan Ross, Professor Emeritus, Robert Quinn).

About this practice

This practice helps a team become clear on why it exists and the needs it serves, by linking 'Why?' and 'What?' with 'So what?' statements. It creates a common or shared reason for the team existing, which helps create a greater sense of belonging – an important goal of the Orientating stage.

It also can help differentiate one team from another, strengthening team identity. If a team lacks the autonomy to decide its purpose, then it's best not to ask them to create it! Instead, ask the team's stakeholders to explain its purpose, then invite the team to bring it to life. This practice, involving the whole team, is based on an approach by former Harvard professor and teams researcher, Ruth Wageman (2019), and can be carried out in-person or virtually.

Time

→ More than 45 minutes – longer if the team is very large in size, or there are subgroups.

→ Send out the 'formula' in advance for team members to prepare (see step 2 below).

What you will need

→ Coloured sticky notes

→ Three flip charts and stands, plus coloured marker pens

→ A note of the purpose 'formula'.

Step-by-step guide

1. Prime this practice by asking the team members to consider the following questions:

    → Why does this team exist?

    → What would be missing if this team didn't exist?

    → What is this team's core work?

    → What is it that only this team can do?

→ What makes us unique?

→ What is this team's contribution to the wider organisation?

2. Introduce the shared purpose formula:

→ Why: 'This team exists to...'

→ What: 'By doing...' – a few bullet points of major tasks or key priorities

→ So what: 'So that...' – what is the impact of the team on the organisation and/or customer?

3. Ask each member to write their answers (individually) on separate sticky notes for each of the three parts of the formula.

4. Put the sticky notes on three different flip charts (one for each part of the formula). Invite the whole team to stand around each flip chart in turn, and identify and group themes together before discussing them. Highlight patterns and ideas that resonate.

5. Now divide the team into three subgroups. Ask each group to take one of the three parts of the purpose formula and write a succinct, final draft (20 minutes).

6. Share the three drafts of each of three subgroup purposes with the whole team.

7. Before finalising this purpose statement, check that it is:

→ inspiring

→ involves input from key stakeholders and/or sponsors

→ really matters

→ provides meaning

→ resonates with each member and the whole team.

Tips on getting the most from this practice

→ I haven't called this practice 'creating' your team's purpose because it already exists. A better description is 'clarifying' your team's purpose – identifying what exists already but being more explicit about it.

→ It's best to keep responses short – the shorter, the better – as this leads to a more compelling purpose statement.

→ Similarly, don't get bogged down in wordsmithing drafts or final purpose statements. A little tidying up is fine, but too much and purpose statements lose their essence.

→ A team's purpose varies depending on who you ask, so it's worth getting input from a range of stakeholders to create a shared picture of success. This could include the leader's manager, dependent teams or customers.

→ A team's purpose can change as the context changes, so it is worthwhile checking and updating it periodically.

Variations

→ A coach can help the team's leader draft the purpose statement and then develop it further with input from the team, or start by clarifying this with the team from the outset. I prefer the latter because it engages the team in the process.

→ If a team is conducting this practice after merging with other teams, it could be carried out with members from across the original teams as a way of helping them come together and form into a new team.

Establishing your team's goals

Objectives trump everything else when it comes to team performance.

Michael West, Professor of Organisational Psychology,
Lancaster University Management School

The work of eminent teams researcher, Michael West, tells us that creating and agreeing team objectives and reviewing them regularly is one of the most positively influential factors for effective team-based working. It positions goal-setting clearly as an enabler of team performance.

What this practice can help with

Goals are crucial for teams: they provide direction, focus attention and let a team know how well they are progressing. Goals also influence who is on the team, particularly if different skills are needed to achieve them, and new members need to be recruited.

Goals direct behaviour, and behaviour drives performance – yet leaders often stop after setting individual goals, and forget to fix team goals. Individual goals reinforce individual contributions, not interdependent, collaborative team behaviour. Goals are vital for teams too, and significant research evidence supports the positive effect that goals have on team performance (see e.g. Tannenbaum and Salas 2021; West and Markiewicz 2016).

About this practice

This practice helps teams set goals. It can be used for newly-forming teams that are deciding their goals, or for established teams which currently have no (clear) goals.

Goals are important at the Orientating stage because they help a team understand the work it must do. The practice starts with a reminder of your team's vision, purpose and stakeholder needs before turning to its work and the priorities.

Time

As the team will be held to account to deliver these goals, it's worth spending time creating them. This practice can take 30–60 minutes.

What you will need

→ Sticky notes to document the tasks to be completed before agreeing goals.
→ Flip charts and marker pens to write out the team goals, so everyone can see them.

This practice can also work just as well virtually

Step-by-step guide

1. Start with the team leader reminding the team about its vision, purpose, stakeholders and their needs.
2. As a team, ask and discuss:

   → What do we need to achieve as a team?
   → How will we know when we have accomplished these?

→ What are our indicators of progress (milestones) and success (measures)?

→ What specific results and deliverables do we need to achieve and by when?

3. Discuss as a team the tasks to be done to achieve the purpose and vision. This could be done together if your team is small, or in smaller groups if the team is large. Express these tasks as team goals.

4. Decide who in the team will do what and when to contribute to the goals.

5. Check that the draft goals are SMART (Specific, Measurable, Achievable, Realistic and Time-bound).

6. Decide what measures the team will use to gauge progress and goal-completion.

7. Discuss these draft goals as a whole team, amending them as needed.

8. Prioritise these goals by importance. Select three top-priority goals.

9. Agree how you will hold each other to account for delivering these goals.

Tips on getting the most from this practice

→ Make your goals:

→ challenging – this leads to higher performance

→ learning-oriented – to help teams find better solutions to complex problems

→ aligned with individual team members' goals – so they are mutually reinforcing.

→ Some example team goals include:

→ working out our success formula as a team

→ understanding the reason we missed last week's performance target

→ working out how we can be even more effective

→ repairing damaged relationships between members.

→ (Optional) Some teams choose to communicate their goals beyond the team: this can increase external motivation and help achieve them.

Variations

Try this variation as you adapt this practice to your team and its needs:

→ Invite stakeholders and/or customers along to a goal-setting session to hear what's important to them directly.

→ Invite each team member to consider their individual goals, and examine these for coherence with the team's goals.

Clarifying team member roles

Collaboration improves when the roles of individual team members are clearly defined.
Tammy Erickson, Executive Fellow, London Business School

This quote explains the importance of team member role clarity. In my experience of coaching teams, when roles are unclear this is often expressed behaviourally and can contribute to significant dysfunction.

What this practice can help with

Teams are formed from people working together. To achieve this requires roles that align, but not overlap – and some careful design. Roles can be either 'who' is on the team, or 'what' tasks these members carry out. We focus on the latter. This practice is important to a newly-forming team where roles can be unclear, and can help to create greater role alignment. It can increase the degree of interdependence between members and sense of being part of 'one team'.

About this practice

The purpose of this practice is to help clarify team roles through a process of negotiation, and can be used with a newly-forming team or to confirm changes to existing roles. Clarifying team roles is important at this stage because it helps individuals understand the work they must do, and avoids duplication and potential clashes through role overlap.

This practice is based on a process that Roger Harrison (2010) called 'role negotiation', created to improve how people work in teams, and involves four phases:

1. Unfreeze – preparing to loosen existing views about roles
2. Negotiate – clarifying mutual expectations about roles, and deciding what belongs to individual members and to the whole or part of a team
3. Closing – deciding how to operationalise the new agreed or changed role
4. Follow up – putting the roles into practice.

Time

→ 'Unfreezing' can take 20+ minutes, and pairs negotiations 30–40 minutes. Allow longer if there is significant role overlap and renegotiation needed.

→ 'My best contribution' can take 20 minutes depending on numbers.

What you will need

→ Ask team members to bring along a copy of their job description.

→ Teams could print copies of Table 7 below to complete. (This practice can work virtually, showing Table 7 on screen.)

Step-by-step guide

The team can prepare for this practice by each member considering the following questions in advance of role 'negotiation':

→ Who is a member of our team?

→ What specific roles do others on the team play?

→ Can my/your role be done by an individual, or does it require a team?

→ (For the team leader) What role is missing that should be part of our team? Which role is not/no longer needed and should not form part of our team?

→ How does my/your role contribute to our team overall?

→ Where would the team benefit, if I were to give something up?

→ What would I need from others in the team to help me achieve my role and goals?

Then, try this approach to role negotiation:

1. Unfreeze – review your team role, major activities or tasks and goals individually. Consider those of other team members.

2. Negotiate – based on these preparations, each team member in turn shares information on their role with another member, with whom they work closely and are reliant on. Team members state the work they can carry out themselves autonomously, and that is the responsibility of the whole (or part of the) team. Use Table 7 below.

3. Be prepared to negotiate the role, aiming to link core tasks and key activities together, and avoiding or renegotiating any overlaps.

4. Close – finalise your negotiations. Agree any changes and a plan to implement them. Check role alignment across the team by sharing the new agreements with the whole team.

5. Follow up – put the clarified roles into practice.

Table 7: Team member–team role negotiation chart

What tasks am I responsible for? (Alone and autonomously)	**What tasks is the team responsible for?** (All or part of the team)
Stakeholder plan	Stakeholder relationships (held by different team members)
Strategic planning (Process)	Strategic plan (as a tangible product)

Tips on getting the most from this practice

→ Agreeing a standard template to help individual members prepare creates a consistent approach across the team.

→ Discussing roles, tasks and goals can be done in pairs, triads or all together. If unsure, start in pairs.

→ 'Negotiate' means giving something up to get something back in return!

→ Be specific when agreeing your new role. Write agreements down.

→ Roles can drift over time. Check these align periodically.

Variations

Team roles also can be the contributions that members are able to make beyond their technical roles. Identifying and drawing on them explicitly can play to their strengths.

'My best contribution to this team'

→ Invite each member in turn to say what their *one* best contribution is to the team. Go beyond obvious functional role-associated contributions.

→ (If time permits) Ask other team members to acknowledge if they have seen this contribution in action. Offer appreciation.

→ Encourage members to limit it to one contribution to save time.

Chapter 5
The Resolving stage

As long as the candle burns, there is time to make repairs.

Israel Salanter, rabbi

In a gentle way, Israel reminds us that there is nearly always time to resolve difficulties in teams, and to take the opportunity to do so.

By the time a team reaches stage 2, it will have been set up and launched successfully:

→ the team will be clear on why it exists, and its common purpose and vision
→ key stakeholders will have been identified, and their needs have begun to be understood
→ members will have begun to get to know one another, and started working together towards shared goals.

Whereas in the Orientating stage team members wanted to fit in with others, in the Resolving stage they seek to become more independent. Whereas beforehand, members sought to be more dependent on others in the team and expressed little dissatisfaction, as their confidence grows, they feel able to push back. They exert their authority, challenge the work, how it is carried out and the leader. This can lead to friction and clashes in a team. The Resolving stage is characterised by members' emotional responses to their tasks and intra-team conflict.

Team goals at the Resolving stage

To progress in its development (and move on to the next, Collaborating, stage), teams will need to work through and achieve the following goals:

→ develop team values, processes and norms to get work done (Practice 13 on page 50)
→ resolve any team conflict arising, especially on role and task overlap(s) and the leader and/or leadership being offered (Practice 15 on page 54)
→ protect team members during disagreements (a key team leader role)
→ channel team members' energies towards work and tasks (see Practice 25: 'Increasing contributions in your team' on page 82).

What teams need at the Resolving stage

This second stage of development presents teams with several challenges, including working through any lack of role and task clarity from the first stage of team development, and ensuing conflict between members.

The work for your team to complete at this stage includes:

→ building (psychological) safety and trust between team members
→ developing team norms and processes.

The Resolving stage practices

The practices for this stage help address these team needs, and include:

→ making sense of and clarifying your team's roles and work to be done
→ handling conflicts and disagreements while remaining resilient.

This is a vital developmental stage for a team: many get stuck and don't progress through it successfully. Stick with it because the teams that do come out the other side are much closer-knit, and far more effective.

Good luck!

Improving dialogue in your team

Dialogue is a living experience of inquiry within and between people.

William Isaacs, Senior Lecturer and Co-founder, Organizational Learning Center, Massachusetts Institute of Technology

This quote emphasises that dialogue is an exchange between people rather than a monologue, as often occurs when one team member argues for their position.

What this practice can help with

Teams engage in complex work requiring collaboration. The skill of conducting effective dialogue enables this, but is underdeveloped in many teams. Dialogue is an exchange between two or more people involving listening and talking, with the aim of discovering something new; Bill Isaacs (1999) thinks of it as a 'shared inquiry'.

Dialogue can help team members identify and understand different perspectives and make sense of them together, avoiding or resolving conflicts. Dialogue that doesn't take place with the whole team tends to lead to separate, side conversations that distract or divide the team. Dialogue is the currency of collaboration.

About this practice

These practices show teams how to improve the quality of their dialogue. This is important at this stage to help teams develop group norms and effective processes. Engaging in constructive dialogue is a sign of psychological safety. Two practices are included.

Time

→ The 'team dialoguing' practice takes 20 minutes per topic.

→ Using the coloured cards practice takes a moment.

What you will need

→ Each person will need a chair to sit on, and the room arranged with the chairs in a circle in the first practice.

→ Individual red, amber and green A5 cards.

This practice can also work just as well virtually.

Step-by-step guide

Both practices can be started by asking, 'What do we need to agree to make it safer to have this conversation?'

Team dialoguing

1. Sit in a circle of individual, equally spaced chairs between team members.
2. Check in (use Practice 4 on page 28) to tune into each other and listen differently.
3. Start a dialogue by agreeing the broad topic area: e.g. 'Mergers'.

4. Provide some context (the team leader or topic sponsor could do this).
5. Then, agree the general focus of the topic area: e.g. 'A potential merger with Acme Inc.'
6. Decide on the specific question the team would like to answer. This is not a stage to rush – identifying the right question is crucial and worth taking time over.
7. Invite team members to answer the question, keeping individual inputs roughly equal (e.g. limited to 2 minutes or three sentences per person).
8. Check out (using Practice 4 again).

Traffic light cards

It's easy for dialogue to get 'blocked' between team members, whether intentionally or not. The use of simple red, amber and green cards can keep a conversation flowing.

1. A team uses a set of coloured cards while meeting.
2. If a team member speaks and uses words that help dialogue flow, members hold up the green card (green for 'Go' on a traffic light).
3. If the same member starts to use language that could lead to blocked dialogue, other members could hold up the amber card (amber to 'Slow Down' or 'Prepare to Stop' on a traffic light). This acts as a visual cue of the observed impact of that member's behaviour, and encourages them to use different language. This can act as a timely reminder to change any limiting behaviour.
4. If a member speaks and uses words that block dialogue, then any member could hold up the red card. The speaking member could recover the conversation if it has stopped and/or restart it.
5. If the team is particularly large, more than one set of cards could be used across the team, so everyone has access to them (if meeting in person). If the team is meeting virtually, each member could use coloured sticky notes.

The power of this practice lies in the immediacy of its feedback through the cards, and the potential to correct language and behaviour quickly. It builds capability in the team by encouraging members to look for behaviours that help or hinder dialogue, and is a psychologically safer way of challenging others' behaviour without using words.

Tips on getting the most from this practice

→ Practise the skill of brevity. Using fewer words makes it easier to listen.
→ Be kind. Words carry meaning, and can be used to wound as well as communicate.
→ 'WAIT': Why Am I Talking? Check your intention before or while speaking.
→ Check for 'hub and spoke' dialogue, where the conversation goes into and out from the team's leader. To improve openness and avoid an overreliance on the team leader to 'manage' conversations, increase the number of exchanges directly between team members. This will also allow the team leader to contribute more to a conversation.
→ It is important that everyone speaks.
→ It is best to agree a 'no interruptions' rule while others are talking.
→ Check for common understanding by asking, 'What did we all hear?'

Creating a team working agreement

No matter what accomplishments you achieve, somebody helps you.

Althea Gibson, American tennis player

We all need someone sometimes – and nowhere is this truer than in teams, where members are reliant on one another. This practice helps team members agree how to help each other.

What this practice can help with

Teams generate great strategies and come up with fantastic ideas to deliver them – then often fail to do just that! A common reason is that they rarely agree on how to work together to achieve their goals.

About this practice

Working agreements are the ongoing ways of behaving, communicating and interacting that guide team members' daily work together. Once practised, they are a route to creating group norms and processes and can help avert any conflict – both important at this stage in the team's maturity.

Creating a clear working agreement turns intentions into reality. They should include how the team will hold themselves and each other accountable for them, and what to do when any agreements are broken. Research on the impact of team charters by academics John Mathieu and Tammy Rapp found that having a high-quality charter was important for performance in the early stages of a team's formation, and helped improve the effects of other team performance strategies. See for yourself.

Description of practice

This practice shows teams how to create a working agreement. It is like the 'ground rules' practice in the Orientating stage (see Practice 6 on page 32). This one differs in that it's co-created with the team: longer term, and based on teams' experience of working together. Once decided, it's everyone's responsibility to follow the agreement.

Time

If considered in advance and the number of agreements kept small, this practice can be done in 20 minutes. If not, allot 40 minutes.

What you will need

No specific materials are needed, although writing the agreements on a flip chart where the whole team can read them can be useful. Type the agreements into a separate document to help teams continue to refer to them. This practice can also work just as well virtually.

Step-by-step guide

1. As a team, discuss and agree how you would like to work together, based on your experience of being a team so far (see examples below). Use any of these questions as prompts:

    → What do we expect of each other in this team?

    → How are we currently working that helps us achieve our goals?

    → How do we need to behave when we are together to deliver our goals?

→ What team behaviours are getting in our way of delivering results?

→ What do I need to change in my behaviour to put these agreements into practice?

→ How can I help other team members put them into practice?

→ How will we hold each other to account to live up to these agreements?

→ What will our action(s) be if team members break the agreements?

2. This practice could be primed by inviting team members to reflect on how they have worked together so far:

→ What has worked well?

→ What is being tolerated that could be better?

3. Invite everyone in the team to contribute to gain maximum buy-in.

4. Check that everyone in the team is willing to agree to the statements.

5. Check progress against the agreement periodically:

→ What's been easily adopted?

→ What's been more difficult, and why?

Tips on getting the most from this practice

→ The use of the word 'agreement' is deliberate, since it's a collaborative experience co-created with team members.

→ Describe the statements behaviourally (e.g. 'We will speak up when we see something that could be improved') – it will be easier to act on them.

→ Keep the statements short. They will be remembered, which makes them easier to put into practice. Some examples:

→ Speak up and have a straight conversation

→ Talk, then agree actions

→ Focus on what we *can* control

→ Build on each other's solutions to problems

→ Reach clear decisions

→ Be accountable – do what you say.

→ Be selective. It is far better to choose three to six behavioural statements and put them into action, than create a longer list and do nothing with it. Ten or more agreements is too many.

→ At some point, a team member will break the working agreement and start to fall back into old routines. This can be an opportunity to remind everyone of the agreement, revising and renewing commitment to it.

Variations

→ For large teams, this practice can be done in subgroups first, before creating a single set of working agreements for the whole team.

→ Working agreements are live documents to be updated regularly. Remove older statements that have become part of the team's routines. Add new ones as necessary. Keep them alive.

Building trust between team members

If you can trust yourself when all men doubt you
But make allowance for their doubting too...

Rudyard Kipling, English poet and writer

Kipling's famous poem tells us how certain things should be done. Try increasing your trustworthiness and building trust in your team, and see what happens.

What this practice can help with

Trust matters in teams where success hinges on teamwork, flexibility, innovation and high degrees of co-operative working, according to team researchers Ana Christina Costa and Neill Anderson (2012) of Brunel University. They focused on team-level collective trust, where team members share a general belief that others are trustworthy.

Trust matters even more where members are dependent on one another in virtual teams, and is even more significant in a team's leadership because it allows teams to accept their leader's actions, goals and decisions reports, advise Kurt Dirks and Donald Ferrin respectively. Trust makes sound economic sense too, says Tony Simons at Cornell University, USA who found that firms whose managers delivered on their promises were found to be 2.5 per cent more profitable.

While definitions of trust vary and are complex, it matters.

About this practice

This practice shows teams how to build trust. This can help stage 2 teams work through disagreements. Research by Roger Mayer of North Carolina State University, USA shows that trust consists of several elements:

→ Ability – does the other person have the skills to do what they say?

→ Altruism – is this person acting in my best interest, versus their own?

→ Integrity – is this person acting with honesty and to a set of values? (Mayer et al. 1995)

David Maister et al. (2002) added two other elements:

→ reliability – delivering on promises

→ intimacy – trustworthiness with confidential information.

I added 'vulnerability' by Patrick Lencioni, author of *The Five Dysfunctions of a Team* (2002), and combined them into a single checklist for these practices.

Time

The mini-practices below give the timings.

What you will need

Copies of the self-score table (Table 8 below) to carry out the trust audit. This practice can work virtually, showing Table 8 on screen.

Step-by-step guide

Start with the first two activities individually or in pairs before trying the variation as a team. In most cases, it will prove too exposing to carry out trust practices successfully in a larger group.

Conduct an individual trust audit

1. As a team member, carry out an individual self-trust audit by rating yourself against the question, 'To what extent...' on a scale of high, medium to low (H, M, L), levels of trust in yourself. This should take you about 15 minutes.
2. Review your scores. Where do you consider yourself the most or least trustworthy?
3. Act on your findings and in ways that increase your trustworthiness, and promote trust in you by others.

Table 8: Self-trust audit

Element	To what extent:	Score (H, M, L)
Ability	Do I have the skills/knowledge to deliver what I have promised the team?	
Altruism	Are my actions serving my own needs, versus those of the team?	
Integrity	Does my reputation show me as truthful and sincere? Do my values promote trust?	
Reliability	Do I consider myself reliable? Do others in the team rely on me?	
Intimacy	Do I maintain confidences? Do I keep privileged information private?	
Vulnerability	Am I willing to be vulnerable, and show it in front of the team? Am I open about both my strengths and limitations with the team?	

Rate and monitor trust in other members of your team

Carry out a team trust audit of your fellow team members using the steps below. This takes 15–20 minutes.

1. Using Table 8, rate each team member on how much you trust them using the same scale.
2. Act on your findings: help others develop their individual trust, and find ways of helping them to trust you more (e.g. by asking them for help).
3. Monitor these trust scores. Notice how different actions change them.

Tips on getting the most from this practice

→ Trust builds over time but can be lost quickly. Take your time.

→ If you want to be trusted, try trusting others first!

→ Build trust by experimenting. Try showing some vulnerability through personal disclosure. Be selective on what you say and to whom, initially. Start small with those you trust. Gauge how team colleagues respond. Increase your disclosure as trust builds.

→ Develop your trustworthiness through actions (e.g. making sure you are consistent, always delivering what you say will) to give team members the evidence you can be trusted.

Variations

PWC's Jon Katzenbach believes the best way to build trust in teams is for the team to engage in real work (Katzenbach and Smith 1993). Identify or create real work opportunities to develop trust. Carry them out. Review and learn from them.

Tackling conflict

You don't get harmony when everybody sings the same note.

Doug Floyd, Co-founder and Producer, Canopy Theatre Company

Floyd's quote challenges us to understand that some disagreement can be healthy.

What this practice can help with

The prevailing opinion is that conflict is a bad thing. MIT's Peter Senge challenges this view in his book *The Fifth Discipline* (1990), saying: 'In great teams conflict becomes productive' (p. 249). He describes conflict as 'a situation in which interdependent people express differences in satisfying their individual needs and interests and experience interference from each other in accomplishing their goals'.

Signs of conflict also signal that something is important to team members. Whether conflict is additive to a team depends on whether it is focused on tasks (e.g. the team's work or how it is carried out), or personal issues (e.g. a team member failing to deliver, or repeatedly showing up late – issues best dealt with in private by the team leader).

Here, we concentrate on task-related conflict.

About this practice

There are no magic wands when it comes to handling conflict. It's a necessary part of stage 2 development. I suggest a team creates a conflict-handling protocol *before* getting into conflict, so it has a way to work through it when it arises (as it will at some point).

Time

If raised early, potential conflict can be handled in minutes. If left to fester, it can take longer (60+ minutes) to work through.

What you will need

If the team has a written working agreement (see Practice 13: 'Creating a team working agreement' on page 50), it can be useful to have a copy available to refer to handy. No other materials are required. This practice can also work just as well virtually.

Step-by-step guide

Start by preparing for this practice:

1. Work within your team's conflict comfort zone. As team leader, gauge this by asking: 'What is my team's current level of comfort with conflict?' You may need to encourage members to verbalise disagreements in some teams while practising more self-restraint in others.
   Then, work through these steps to agree the procedure:

2. As the leader, start by reminding everyone that conflict is necessary and an important part of improving team effectiveness. Add that avoiding conflict can damage it.

3. Check there is sufficient psychological safety, particularly if there is (or appears to be) a reluctance to discuss conflict. Ask the team, 'How can we make it safe for us all to discuss this conflict?'

4. As a team, reflect on a time when you were in conflict.

5. Discuss the following questions, aiming to build up a detailed picture of what the conflict was about, how it occurred and how the team handled it.

   → **When** did the conflict occur? On what time/day/month?

   → Was there a series of conflict episodes? Over what period/duration?

   → **Where** did the conflict occur – what was the setting?

   → **What** was the conflict about?

   → **Who** was (or was not) involved; what roles did people play?

   → **Why** did the conflict happen? (There could be different perceptions, so ask everyone involved).

   → **How** did it happen: what was the sequence of events, who did what?

   → **What** was the impact? How did the conflict affect the people involved? What was the effect on the whole team, and those outside it?

   → **What's next?** How did the conflict end; was it resolved? What was agreed would happen next (if anything)? What would team members like to happen now to resolve the conflict?

   → Check for contributions from everyone in the team to achieve closure.

6. A leader has the greatest influence on psychological safety. How safe are you making it in your team? Thank team members for alternative viewpoints – even if you believe they are not useful. Accept differences openly. Admit your errors and limits to role model for others.

7. It is important everyone speaks. Gather input by saying, 'It's important we hear from everyone. What other views are there on this for us to consider as a team?' This ensures everyone's voice is heard, brings more diversity of thought and supports resolution.

8. Many disagreements are seen as being conflicts of interest, whereas often they are about unmet needs. Team members can help each other by asking, 'What need is not being met?', or 'What do you need here?'

9. Don't forget to ask for *your* needs to be met by others in the team, e.g. 'I get concerned if I don't know what's going on. I then try to control things. Please update me first so I don't need to ask.'

10. By now you should be clearer on what causes conflict in your team. Agree how you will respond when conflict arises using 'If... then...' sentences, e.g.: 'If Tom starts to argue for his own budget to be ring-fenced at risk to others' projects, then Baljit will call this out, and Nancy will remind everyone about our agreed team behaviours.'

Be specific about who will do what.

11. Take a break if the conversation is getting heated (5 minutes can suffice), or if time is needed to gather missing facts.

12. Having worked through the conflict, check the impact on team member relationships. Repair any harm done (e.g. acknowledge there were disagreements, offer an apology).

13. Identify individual and team learning. Update the team's task processes and working agreement.

14. As team leader, thank everyone who contributed for their efforts – especially anyone who, for example, took a risk by offering a new approach (regardless of whether it was adopted).

Tips on getting the most from this practice

→ Conflict is rarely discussed in teams despite being common. Leaders can help teams deal with conflict by talking about and normalising it.

→ Small things can become big things. Nip them in the bud with early action.

Naming 'the elephants in the room'

Primum non nocere [Above all else, do no harm].

Misattributed to Hippocrates and the Hippocratic Oath

Group dynamics can have a harmful effect on teams. The Hippocratic Oath reminds us not to compound this when working with dynamics.

What this practice can help with

Most teams will encounter group dynamics between members at some point, especially at the Resolving stage of development. A dynamic might be explained as the way that two or more people behave with each other in a team because of a particular context.

Teams can find dynamics slippery to grab hold of, and tricky to handle. While they might have the commitment to confront these, they often lack the skills to do so effectively.

About this practice

This practice is a simple but effective and safe way for teams to name and work through a tricky dynamic. Called 'Naming the elephant in the room', the Russian poet, Ivan Krylov, popularised it in 1814 into the now widely-known aphorism. It can help protect team members while working through a potentially difficult subject to raise.

American team consultant Bennett Bratt suggests a simple four-step approach to working with group dynamics (p. 70):

1. See it
2. Name it
3. Own it
4. Work it

We have assumed here that the team is aware of a challenging dynamic, and so this practice focuses on naming it – labelling it to make it easier for them to raise and discuss. Sometimes, just doing this can be enough to take the energy out of it and settle it. Owning a dynamic means taking responsibility for it: it's best if the whole team does this, rather than one team member, to avoid scapegoating them.

Working on a dynamic means working through it. Dynamics are not problems to be solved; rather, more a source of data that tells you something important about the team. (Dynamics are discussed further in the Appendix.)

Time

Allow 30–40 minutes for each of these practices.

What you will need

→ A5 postcards or sheets of foldable paper
→ Coloured marker pens
→ Copies of the team's ground rules and/or working agreements, if created.

This practice will need adapting to work virtually safely.

Step-by-step guide

This practice is like one developed by Gestalt practitioner John Leary-Joyce, which he calls 'Naming the dead dog' in his book, *The Fertile Void* (2014).

1. Make it sufficiently psychologically safe to discuss 'elephants' in the team. (A check-in can help – see Practice 4 on page 28).
2. Provide each team member with a piece of paper and marker pens.
3. Invite team members to write one undiscussable topic on a piece of paper, then fold it up and place it into a container (a box or bowl).
4. Ask team members to pick one folded piece of paper and read the contents aloud, as if it were their own topic.
5. Expand on the topic with examples from their own experience.
6. Encourage team members to express how they feel about the topics, as well as what they think about them, to release any pent-up frustrations.
7. Shift the conversation from describing the dynamic to possible solutions and actions by asking each other these questions:

    → What impact is this dynamic having on us as a team?

    → What might we want to do about the dynamic?

8. Invite the team to talk about what they have learned from their conversation.

Tips on getting the most from this practice

→ Avoid blaming, shaming or scapegoating any individual team member or the leader.

→ Agree ground rules first to create enough safety for the practice.

→ Remember the Hippocratic Oath: aim to do no harm when working with dynamics.

→ Avoid blaming individual team members by not writing their names on the cards.

→ Writing on cards in capital letters can anonymise individuals' comments.

→ Encourage teams to use the F-word – feelings! This makes it normal to discuss how team members experience something. Try asking another team member, 'What is going on for you (now)?'

Variations

Replace steps 3–4 above with the following variation:

→ Ask each team member to write down the top three items that the team needs to talk about, and topics that are undiscussable. Ask: 'What topics are undiscussable in this team?'

    → Gather the cards together and shuffle them to mix the contributions.

    → Inviting members to work as a team, place the cards in a continuum, from most easily discussed to most undiscussable topics.

    → Group cards into similar themes.

    → Ask the team to select the three most undiscussable topics before discussing each of them in turn, with the team deciding the order.

→ This practice could be used with Practice 31: 'Identifying your team's rackets' (on page 98). Start with this practice (to name dynamics), then follow it with the rackets practice to understand and start to change them.

Helping your team build critical moment resilience

Resilient teams are just as important to businesses as resilient individuals...
the payoff is organisations and teams that are built to last.

Bradley Kirkman, Professor of Leadership, North Carolina State University

There is significant focus on building resilient individuals, but we hear far less about building resilient teams despite the benefits.

What this practice can help with

Teams face innumerable challenges that require resilience, including: time pressures, difficult assignments, insufficient resources, 'crisis' events, continuous low-level pressures, and so on (Alliger et al. 2015). What team isn't facing at least one of these?

Psychologist George Alliger tells us that 'resilience is the capacity to withstand and recover from challenges, pressure, or stressors', and that it operates at both the whole team and individual team member levels.

Having a group of resilient individuals doesn't always translate into a resilient team. A classic response is for teams to 'learn to toughen up'. While this may help them get through one tough time, it doesn't help build capacity to respond to repeated instances or remain viable while sustaining performance.

These practices help teams with this.

About this practice

These practices show teams how to create, maintain and improve their resilience. They focus on 'critical moments': moments that really matter to a team, such as holding their nerve under pressure during a key investor pitch or delivering a high-performance project. They are developed from the work of Olympic sport performance psychologist, Dr Steve Bull.

For teams at the Resolving stage, this also can build their capacity to withstand and recover from challenges associated with working through disagreements, differences and conflicts. Critical moment resilience requires clear thinking and a positive focus. This practice shows teams how to achieve this.

Time

→ Celebrating the team's successes can take 10–30 minutes.

→ Allot 60 minutes to identify the team's 'success formula'.

→ Allow time to prepare for 'Control the controllables', and 20 minutes for the practice.

→ Building on the positives can be as quick as 3 minutes if done often.

What you will need

Flip chart and marker pens. This practice can also work just as well virtually.

Step-by-step guide

With all these practices, as a team, ask: 'What actions can we take individually and collectively as a team to minimise (anticipate), manage (during) and mend (afterwards) instances where we need more resilience?'

Celebrate team successes

Recent and past achievements can be easily forgotten or neglected, with a focus on current challenges – yet discussing past successes can improve team potency (a general belief in the team's capabilities).

1. Discuss prior successes as a team.

   → What did the team achieve?

   → What was significant about it that made it a stand-out success?

2. How did the team recognise this achievement – how was it rewarded?

3. It's not too late to recognise great work. Find a way to celebrate now.

Identify the team's 'success formula'

How teams work can become routine quickly, and easily forgotten or underestimated ('It was nothing; it's just the way we do things.') This practice makes explicit what a team does well, so that these actions be repeated more intentionally and frequently. One way to do this is for teams to identify their 'success formula': establish what they have done in the past which led to their being successful. As a team, ask:

1. What did the team do to achieve its successes? What role did team members play? Write them down.

2. Turn these team routines into task processes. Update existing team procedures. Who did what in what order? Who collaborated with whom?

Build on the positives

It is easy to dwell on the negatives. Focus on the positives instead.

Make explicit anything that helped, and is helping, the team succeed, e.g. a new joining member brings extra capacity, acquisition of new skills after training. Notice the small things as well as the bigger items. Build on them.

Control the controllables

Decide what is inside and outside the team's ability to control and influence. Try to avoid worrying about the latter.

1. Make separate lists of 'controllable' and 'uncontrollable' factors. Focus on the 'controllables'. Discuss how the team will keep these in mind, and how it can avoid being distracted by items that are uncontrollable.

2. Separate processes (doing) from performance (achievement): i.e. if a team stays focused on its work, performance should take care of itself.

Tips on getting the most from this practice

→ Display team achievements visually to remind everyone of them.

→ Disappointments and frustrations abound at work. Get into the practice of looking for the good stuff too. Amplify the positives to set the tone.

→ Being present will focus the team on the present. Watch if it drifts.

Variations

Be more mindful. Mindfulness techniques help teams stay present. Start by simply taking deep breaths to control faster breathing rates when the team is under pressure.

Chapter 6
The Collaborating stage

In the long history of humankind – those who have learned to collaborate
and improvise most effectively have prevailed.

Attributed to Charles Darwin, English naturalist, geologist and biologist

Darwin reminds us that we have evolved only by having learned to work together. If teams wish to prevail, they will likely need to do the same.

After the conflictual challenges of the Resolving stage, the Collaborating stage will seem more straightforward. Teams will have developed the methods, trust and resilience to work through conflict, and the skills to hold constructive dialogue. The team's goals and work are clearer, its communication being open and task-focused, with team members being willing to exchange views more freely without fear of sparking disagreements with other members or the leader.

However, this is not to say this stage is easy or without its own challenges. Development of group cohesion is the primary task at this stage, so a team can become 'more than the sum of its parts' (to misquote Aristotle), delivering collective outputs to a common purpose.

Team goals at the Collaborating stage

To progress in its development (and move onto the next, Achieving, stage), teams will need to work through and achieve the following goals:

→ negotiate team member roles, priorities and processes (e.g. decision making)
→ develop positive team member relations – group cohesion (or 'team glue').

What teams need at the Collaborating stage

This third stage of development presents teams with several challenges, including working out how to collaborate.

The work for teams to complete at this stage includes:

→ developing levels of trust and 'relational strength' between members (see Practice 14: 'Building trust between team members' on page 52)
→ increasing connections within and between teams (see Practice 23: 'Aligning your team' on page 74)
→ encouraging collective ownership of tasks (see Practice 25: 'Increasing contributions in your team' on page 82) and more distributed or shared leadership
→ watching out for Rob Cross's (Professor of Global Leadership at Babson College) famous 'collab-

orative overload', and burnout (see Practice 33: 'Preventing your team from burning out' on page 102)

→ working through competing priorities and contested resource allocation.

The Collaborating stage practices

The practices for this stage help pull a team together to collaborate more. This cohesion is important to help a team address the increased demands on it as it moves into the next two stages.

Good luck!

Forming a collaboration blueprint

Working together always works. It always works. Everybody has to be on the team.
They have to be interdependent with one another.

Alan Mullaly, CEO of Boeing, then Ford

One of the distinguishing features of a team is the interdependence between members. Ford's Alan Mullaly stresses its significance. Without it, a team is a group of disparate members, and attempts to get them to work intact are unlikely to succeed.

What this practice can help with

By their very nature, teams are groups of interdependent people who deliver collective outputs: their members need to rely on each other, to work together effectively. This is easier said than done, and teams often underestimate the amount of co-operation needed to achieve anything significant (Hogan 2007).

About this practice

Teams may intend to work together, but this doesn't always happen. This practice shows teams how to collaborate. Research shows that teams that do are likely to be more positive and have cohesive relationships – a primary goal at this stage. Collaboration in action is how team members behave towards others as they deliver collective work.

This practice builds on Practice 9: 'Clarifying the team's shared purpose' (page 38). It starts with asking about the team's purpose because it may not be necessary to collaborate on everything: this helps separate what needs to be done together from individuals' tasks.

There is no easy prescription for how teams collaborate. This practice helps teams work out how to do this themselves by focusing on solutions (rather than problems) to current and future collaboration opportunities.

Time

→ This practice takes 30-40 minutes. Add 20 minutes' preparation time.

→ Working out whether and how to collaborate takes time. Make it count!

→ Streamline teamwork processes to optimise collaboration efforts.

What you will need

No specific materials are needed for this practice. This practice can also work just as well virtually.

Step-by-step guide

1. Prepare for this practice as a team by working through the following questions first:

    → What are our highest priorities as a team?

    → Which are the most urgent and/or important?

    → Is our team focused on these or other priorities?

    → What are the expectations about collaborating in our team?

    → Who are this team's most active collaborators?

→ How much time are we spending on working with others?

→ How efficient are our collaborations?

→ How can we improve them?

Then continue with this collaboration practice:

2. For each potential collaboration opportunity, ask:

→ What is our common purpose?

→ Do we need to collaborate on this or is it an individual task?

3. Team members will only collaborate if it helps them, too. As a team member, ask: 'How can collaborating make it easier for *me* to achieve my tasks?'

4. Trust is an important precondition to collaboration: no trust, no collaboration. As a team member, ask yourself: 'How do I know other team members are trustworthy? Am I?' (Check these using the self and team trust audits in Practice 14 on page 52).

5. Views on how to collaborate vary, and can become the cause of conflict. Seek clarity. As a team, ask members, 'What does collaboration look like in practice here?' Discuss and agree this. Write your answers down on a flip chart. Refine them.

6. Many teams want to collaborate, but run out of the energy to try something new. Make it easy: replicate instead of creating something new. As a team ask:

→ Where and how are we already collaborating well?

→ What can we learn from this and use elsewhere?

7. Identify past and current collaboration successes. Analyse them.

8. Using the team's answers from steps 5 and 6 (above), create a team collaboration blueprint: decide who will do what, and in what order. Identify new collaboration opportunities and apply the blueprint to them.

9. Refine the team's collaboration blueprint after your experience of working with others.

Tips on getting the most from this practice

→ Being clear on your team's purpose and checking whether collaborative work requests contribute to achieving this can help the team decide what to take on.

→ Be selective: collaborate on work giving everyone the most impact.

→ Collaborative activities have increased by more than 50 per cent over the past 20 years, according to collaboration expert Rob Cross. It's okay to say 'no' to excessive collaboration requests. Leaders may need to give permission for this.

→ Leaders can also help collaborators by prioritising demands, particularly if they come from outside of the team.

→ Team members copy their leader's behaviour. Are you collaborating? If you want more collaboration as a leader, do it first, say professors Herminia Ibarra and Morten Hansen (2011) of London Business School and University of California, Berkeley, respectively.

Variations

→ Try online collaboration tools (such as Slack or Trello) to improve efficiency.

→ Task team members with hunting for collaboration success stories from across the organisation and elsewhere. Share, learn and try them.

Creating a decision-making protocol

You make better decisions through collaboration.

John Chambers, former Chair and CEO, Cisco Corporation

What this practice can help with

Teams often start conversations without a clear idea about how they will make important decisions. Wishing to be inclusive, they attempt to make decisions by consensus, with everyone agreeing. This is hard and slow to achieve, particularly in larger teams; it also can lead to suboptimal decisions and significant frustration about the decision itself as well as how it has been achieved.

Alternatively, the team leader makes the decision on behalf of the team, then involves members in a conversation, sometimes without their being aware that a decision has been reached already. This can be disengaging for team members when they realise this. However, there are different ways to do things. It can help if teams decide how they will make decisions *before* they get into the substance and content of a decision.

About this practice

Teams unable to reach a decision tend to be less aligned and cohesive, and this can slow or stop them from progressing to the next stage of development. This practice can help your team agree how it will make decisions. The approach to decision making will vary, depending on:

→   the topic and decision to be reached

→   your team's norms

→   the team leader's preferences.

Here are some alternative approaches to decision making (Table 9).

Table 9: Team decision-making approaches (Adapted from Kierson 2009)

Approach	Team leader's role	Team member's role
Directive	The leader makes the decision and informs the team.	Minimal/no input from the team.
Testing	The leader has reached a decision, and tests it with the team before finalising it.	Members input ideas and 'test' the decision but cannot change it.
Consulting	The leader discusses proposals with the team before reaching a decision.	Members input ideas and discuss proposals that may change the decision reached.
Delegation	The team leader gives responsibility to the team. The leader may input ideas.	The team is responsible for the decision. They may consult the leader.
Voting	The whole or an agreed number of the team decides. The team leader manages the voting process, and may vote.	Votes for a/the decision.
Consensus	To gain inputs from all team members. The leader gains agreement from everyone in the team.	Inputs equally and agrees with the decision made by the team.

Time

The time for this practice depends on the complexity of the decision to be made. If your team normally takes a long time to decide, try deciding in a pre-agreed, shorter time. Be disciplined!

What you will need

It can be useful to print out and have a copy of Table 9 available. This practice can work virtually, showing Table 9 on screen.

Step-by-step guide

1. Clarify the topic and decision to be reached. For example, ask:

   → What decision do we need to reach on this topic?

   → What might be difficult about this decision for us?

2. (Team leader) Choose a decision-making process from the table.
3. (Team leader) Think about the specific contribution and inputs you want from the team.
4. Frame the decision as a question (see Tips).
5. Engage in a conversation and reach a decision!
6. Try a range of decision-making methods, followed by a team discussion of how each felt and how useful each method was.

Tips on getting the most from this practice

→ Framing a decision as a question helps make team members' contributions more active.

→ Consider the team's existing authority and power structures, rather than assuming all decisions can be made by consensus.

→ Voting can equalise the power in a team, which may not always lead to the optimal outcome. A weighted decision approach, acknowledging the current distribution of authority, might be better in some situations.

Variations

→ Test to see how robust your team's decision-making process is. Try this variation to reveal differences between team members on a decision made. It can show a lack of clarity on a decision, even when members believe they are aligned.

→ It takes 5 minutes and is a check, so make it quick!

1. Involve all team members in this, after having reached a decision about a topic.
2. On a piece of paper, write down a number showing how clear you are on the decision just made by your team (where 0 = not clear and 10 = completely clear).
3. Fold the piece of paper with your answer and place into a container.
4. On another piece of paper, write down *verbatim* the decision your team has just made. Place this into another container.
5. One team member collects the folded pieces of paper from the container and calculates the mean average of team members' decision clarity scores. Display or read this aloud.
6. Individually, pick up a piece of paper from the container (other than your own) and read out loud the *verbatim* answer to the team's decision on that paper to the team. Repeat this until every team member has read another member's answer.
7. Check for consistency and alignment across the team.

'Five-finger voting' decision making

You've got to vote, vote, vote, vote. That's it; that's the way we move forward.
Michelle Obama, attorney, author and former First Lady of the United States of America

Teams can reach a deadlock and get stuck when making decisions. Voting is one way that they can move beyond this.

What this practice can help with
Teams can find decision making tricky, particularly with emotive topics where opinions and decisions can be divided. The team leader wants to gauge the opinion of everyone in the team, but there isn't long to reach a decision.

Voting can be a useful practice for speedy decision making.

About this practice
The purpose of this practice is to help your team to reach a quick decision. This is a key skill for teams to acquire and develop now to help with through the Achieving and Excelling stages later. Teams can use this voting practice, having decided that it's the best means of reaching a decision (See Practice 19: 'Creating a decision-making protocol' on page 66 for the different methods available).

This practice is also called 'Fist to Five' (the source is unknown).

Time
Voting can be quick and take 1–3 minutes, longer if discussion is needed.

What you will need
Team members will need to use a free hand with five fingers in this practice, or be provided with an alternative means of showing their numerical vote. This practice can also work just as well virtually.

Step-by-step guide
The team leader decides the team will use 'voting' to make a decision.

1.   After a decision has been proposed, each team member casts their vote by holding up the chosen number of fingers on one hand, as follows:

   → No fingers – fold: you want to block the proposal because you believe it is damaging to the team.
   → One finger: you have serious reservations about the decision, but will not block or undermine it. You are willing to state your reservations openly to help others understand them.
   → Two fingers: you have important reservations about the decision, but will still support it.
   → Three fingers: you're fully on board with the decision.

→ Four fingers: you give strong support to the decision and commit to actively participating in it, but are not willing to lead it.

→ Five fingers: you're all in, prepared to own the decision and follow-on project and will take the lead on it, if required.

2. If there are three or more fingers held up by everyone in the team, the team can proceed with the decision.

3. If two fingers are held up by one or more team members, it can be useful to continue the conversation to understand individuals' concerns more fully. This could be continued as a group (if time is available and it's sufficiently psychologically safe to do so), or offline in the form of one-to-one conversations. Questions to ask to understand different views include:

→ Can you say why you see this differently to help us understand?

→ What do we need to discuss to move us closer to agreeing?

4. If there are one or more team members 'folding' (no fingers held up), the team may benefit from a separate meeting to discuss the topic in more depth. This could be preceded by individual conversations between team leader and folding team members first.

Tips on getting the most from this practice

→ It is okay to 'fold'. Disagreeing is an important part of decision making. This practice makes it explicit, rather than going 'underground' and subverting progress later through passive agreement at the decision-making stage.

→ It can be worth checking early in the process whether the team is ready for consensus or a vote, to save time.

→ Asking only those team members who raise an objection to speak can save a lot of time.

→ If a decision requires more thought, fix a date to review it to avoid drift.

→ A transition to consensus decision making is relatively straightforward after this practice has been used for a while.

→ It is possible that this process never ends up with everyone at the three-finger stage – at which point a decision will be required whether to invest more energy to try and shift the voting (e.g. by creating other options), or to move to a different decision-making process in this case.

Variations

→ If it is not psychologically safe enough in the team to vote openly, team members could cast their vote by writing the number of fingers (0–5) they would hold up on a piece of paper. These can be folded up, put into a container and the scores read out anonymously by a team member.

→ The same process can be used in a non-binding way to inform other decision-making processes (e.g. 'Testing').

Identifying on-task, off-task and anti-task behaviours in your team

Coming together is a beginning. Keeping together is progress. Working together is success.

Henry Ford, American industrialist, business magnate and founder of the Ford Motor Company

It is easy to form a team, and far harder to work together. Henry Ford reminds us that doing so can be considered a success.

What this practice can help with

Despite their best endeavours, team members' behaviour sometimes diverts them away from their intended focus and plans. At their best, team behaviours can be 'on-task', leading the team directly towards achieving their goals.

However, teams that aren't clear on their primary task are likely either to engage in 'off-task' work contrary to the team's purpose, or to dilute the team's efforts with different members working on different perceived primary tasks. Worse still, sometimes teams can engage in 'anti-task' actions in complete contradiction to their intentions. This normally occurs when teams are unclear about their primary task, and anxieties exist (e.g. there is a lack of clarity over the team's purpose, roles or leadership), and these unconscious influences can lead to anti-task, self-sabotaging behaviours.

It can be tricky for teams to correct off-task behaviours, particularly when they are fully engaged in their work. Sometimes harder still to spot are anti-task behaviours, as they can be out of active awareness.

About this practice

The aim of this practice is to help your team members quickly, safely and easily identify behaviours and activities that are taking the team off track. This practice improves team processes and helps teams to remain cohesive.

Here are two practices that can help your team members stay on-task:

Time

→ This practice can take seconds if cards are used; longer if using words.

→ Off-task and anti-task activities called out may merit a discussion. Allow time (say 20 minutes) for this, particularly anti-task behaviours, as they may not be evident at first.

What you will need

→ At least one set of A5 red, amber and green cards. They could be laminated for future use. The team may want two to three sets of cards, if there are lots of members, to make them quick to use.

→ Coloured sticky notes work as well as A5 cards. These can be easier for team members to obtain and use if working online or virtually.

This practice can work well virtually, showing the cards on screen.

Step-by-step guide

These practices are best used if the team is aware, or made aware, that it is engaging in off-task or anti-task behaviours. Prepare for this practice as a team by asking the following three questions:

→ What is our primary task as a team?

→ What is our purpose as a team? (See Practice 9: 'Clarifying the team's shared purpose' on page 38.)

→ What do our stakeholders require of this team? (See Practice 24: 'Understanding stakeholder needs' on page 80.)

Words-based practice

1. If the team starts to engage in off-task activities, then any member can ask, 'Are we off-task?' to prompt the team to check and correct its focus.

2. If the team becomes aware it is engaged in anti-task work, any team member can ask, 'Are we engaging in anti-task activities/behaviour?'

3. Finally, if a team is engaged in goal-focused work, any team member can say, 'We are engaged in on-task work' to maintain this focus.

Card-based practice

1. This practice can be used during a team meeting or project review session. The team will need the set of coloured cards available.

2. If a team is engaged in goal-focused work, any team member can hold up the green card. The team carries on with this work.

3. If the team starts to engage in off-task activities, any member can hold up the amber card as a prompt. This acts as a visual cue, and can be a timely reminder to check and correct the work the team is doing.

4. Finally, if the team becomes aware it is engaged in anti-task work, any team member can hold up the red card.

Calling out that the team is on-task can be a useful follow-up to show that it is back on track.

Tips on getting the most from this practice

→ This practice works because of its simplicity. Keep it simple!

→ You can find out more about on-task, off-task and anti-task behaviours in psychoanalyst Dr Anton Obholzer's and Vega Roberts' 1994 book, The Unconscious at Work.

→ Note that a team's primary task can change as the external environment changes. Teams are advised to check for differences between the formal or official primary task, the tasks that others in the organisation believe they exist to carry out, and the work that team members are actually carrying out.

Generating creative ideas by 'brainwriting'

Discard your memory; discard the future tense of your desire; forget them both, both what you knew and what you want, to leave space for a new idea.

Wilfred Bion, English psychoanalyst

This quote links Bion's pioneering work with groups with creativity and the idea of creating more space for new ideas to emerge. Teams could do this by simplifying their busy agendas and creating more time to think.

What this practice can help with

Teams are often faced with finding new ways of doing things, and generating fresh ideas is a great place to start. The most common approach to creating new ideas is 'brainstorming', which operates on the premise that doing this in groups with others will lead to more ideas, and that more ideas are better.

While widely used and extremely popular, research has shown that brainstorming doesn't work, advises Argentinian psychologist and Chair of Business Psychology at University College London, Tomas Chamorro-Premuzic (2015): instead, teams defer to the leader or expert.

About this practice

This practice takes the essence of brainstorming – generating ideas through contributions from multiple people – without the usual pitfalls. 'Brainwriting' is a straightforward way of creating and sharing new ideas in your team; it is based on an activity developed by Horst Geschke, featured in Gray et al.'s 2010 book, *Gamestorming*.)

Time

→ Allow 40–45 minutes for this practice. Writing on cards can take more than 20 minutes.

→ Teams tend to take the time given to them here, so reduce the time to encourage quicker responses.

What you will need

→ Flip chart and coloured marker pens

→ A5 index cards

→ Coloured sticky notes.

This practice can work virtually using member-member chat (instead of cards).

Step-by-step guide

1. Write the name of the topic you wish to generate new ideas for as a header at the top of a flip chart.

2. Give out index cards to everyone in the team, asking them to write one idea per card relating to the subject on the flip chart header.

3. Use the following questions to stimulate new thinking and ideas to help with step 2:

   → What are my newest ideas about this topic?

→ If I had to challenge myself, what more would I say about this topic?

→ What hasn't been thought about or said yet?

→ What are the wildest ideas I have about this topic?

→ If we were to join up ideas, what new possibilities would that create?

4. After writing the idea on the card, pass it to another member of the team and ask them to add their own idea to it, sparked by other ideas on the card.

5. Keep passing the cards around and adding other suggestions until there are several ideas on each card.

6. Once sufficient ideas have been generated on each card, gather in the cards and attach them to the flip chart.

7. Review and discuss the ideas as a whole team, marking the most stand-out ones to be followed up.

Tips to get the most from this practice

→ Subsequent ideas written on a particular card can be enhancements or variations on the original idea, or new, related suggestions.

→ Idea-writing also can be done in silence to avoid the practice being dominated by more talkative team members.

→ Generating ideas before critiquing them is likely to stimulate more ideas.

Variations

This additional practice (called 'Reverse It' by user experience designer, Donna Spencer, in Gray et al. 2010) can be used if teams have become stuck and are finding it tricky to generate new ideas. It takes 30–40 minutes using the same equipment.

→ In small groups of three to four team members, describe the anti-problem – i.e. the opposite of the main problem – for example, for a potential organisational acquisition, the anti-problem would be not making the takeover.

→ Exaggerate the differences between the problem and anti-problem for maximum effect.

→ Write the name of the anti-problem at the top of a flip chart.

→ Generate ideas to solve the anti-problem. Aim for lots of ideas to unstick the status quo. Use any of the questions in step 3 (in the main practice above) to prompt new thinking and further ideas. Write these ideas on sticky notes – one idea per note.

→ Use images, pictures and drawings, so that words become less of a blocker to idea creation.

→ Place the sticky note ideas on the flip chart. As a team, discuss the ideas, grouping similar ones together. Ask, 'What stands out?', 'What is common?'

→ Examine the resultant ideas for insights that could inform or even solve the original problem.

Aligning your team

Sticks in a bundle are unbreakable.

Kenyan proverb

This proverb conjures up an image of pencils that are easily snapped individually, but immensely strong when bunched together. The same is true for teams. Align team members to create strength in unity.

What this practice can help with

For teams to achieve shared goals, it requires them to be aligned. Many teams find this hard to do, and harder still to remain aligned.

About this practice

This practice can help your team become aligned, so its members all contribute to the same ends. It is relevant to teams at this Collaborating stage, and especially valuable to executive teams, linking their vision to the overall organisational vision.

The practice draws on the work of Miles Kierson, an American management consultant specialising in team alignment, and his ExecuTAP process. Kierson defines an aligned team as one that is completely committed to its vision, where each member can be counted on to do their part.

Team alignment is an active process that invites each team member to 'own' a decision made completely, as if it was their own. Where team members are not aligned, the active nature of this process means it is far more visible as opposed to lurking underground: this reduces the risk of subsequent sabotage, as well as providing cues to seek clarification on any reticence. Once understood, steps can be taken to reach alignment.

To become aligned, your team must be clear on its vision already. (Use Practice 8: 'Creating a compelling team vision' on page 36 to help with this.)

Time

This practice can take a few minutes if a team aligns easily; longer, if further dialogue is needed. Teams get quicker aligning through practice.

What you will need

No specific materials are needed for this practice. Sharing material with the team upfront can help a team align over more complex decisions. This practice can also work just as well virtually.

Step-by-step guide

1.   The team engages in dialogue to reach a decision on a given topic. *Before* making the final decision, the leader checks alignment by asking the team:

→   If I make that decision, would anyone in the team not be able to align with it?

→   Is anyone in this team not willing to own this decision we have made?

2.   Each team member in turn says, 'I am aligned,' or 'I am not yet fully aligned.' Questions for each team member to ask themselves include:

→   What will it take for me to align with and own this decision fully?

→   Who and what will need to change here?

→   What will I need to change in my behaviour to align with the team?

→   Am I willing to do that?

3.   If a team member is not yet fully aligned, they then say what they would need to happen to become aligned.

4.   If a team cannot agree to align on a decision, open the dialogue for further discussion to understand concerns more fully.

5.   Once the decision is made, it is every team member's job to own the decision, support it and make it work.

6.   Team members can coach each other at times when they become aware that one or more team members' behaviours are inconsistent with the aligned decision. It's important that this is seen as a collective responsibility, not just the leader's role.

7.   If it becomes apparent that the decision isn't producing the desired results, the process should be reopened to ensure an overt and active response, rather than creating the conditions for an undermining, silent withdrawal of support.

Tips to get the most from this practice

→   It must be possible for teams not to be aligned for them to become aligned!

→   Your team will not become aligned if a member holds on to their individual position, despite a decision having been reached and an agreement made to align to it. It's important to let go when it is time to be aligned in service of the whole team. If this is not possible, then it's best raised at the time, and disagreements explored further.

→   It's better for non-alignment to be out in the open. Maintaining psychological safety is important, so that team members aren't afraid to say they are not aligned.

→   By agreeing to be aligned, a team is committing to an imagined future. This may take some courage, especially if that future is different from the present reality. Team members' willingness to align may depend on the plan to achieve this, so test it by asking as a team:

→   What is the team's plan to implement the decision?

→   Do we have the resources and time needed to put this into place?

→   How confident are we that the team will succeed in making the change?

→   Check for alignment often, as teams do become misaligned over time.

Chapter 7
The Achieving stage

You can't build a reputation on what you are going to do.

Henry Ford, American industrialist, business magnate and
founder of the Ford Motor Company

Intentions and plans are important, but Henry Ford goads us into action with this quote. Results count – and that is the main goal of the Achieving stage.

To have reached this stage of development, teams will have worked out how to operate together, and are now aligned and working towards the same end. The Achieving stage sees teams become effective, productive and delivering results. Their members are clear about the team's goals, and work interdependently to realise them. Having resolved earlier difficulties, the teams focus their energy and collective efforts on achieving results. Both the quality and quantity of work evolves throughout this stage.

Team goals at the Achieving stage

To progress in its development (and move onto the next, Excelling, stage), teams will need to work through and achieve the following goals:

→ continue to develop team effectiveness, which allows them to get the job done and done well
→ make more informed decisions (e.g. about the team's work)
→ remain cohesive and united
→ maintain focus on the outcomes and results of collective work.

What teams need at the Achieving stage

This fourth stage of development presents sees teams continuing to improve their ways of working, so they can carry on delivering great work.

The work for teams to complete at this stage includes:

→ focusing on high-quality and quantity delivery of (outputs) work (see Practice 25: 'Increasing contributions in your team', on page 82)
→ seeking, gathering and providing feedback, and monitoring team performance
→ encouraging information-sharing and collective decision making (see Practices 12, 19 and 20 on pages 48, 66 and 68 respectively)
→ continuing to improve team effectiveness (see Practice 37: 'Evaluating your team's effectiveness', on page 114).

Teams that are unable to learn, improve and deliver more will find themselves stuck at this stage.

The Achieving stage practices

Achieving stage practices help teams respond to these needs: they vary from gathering stakeholder input to inform their work, to focusing on productivity and establishing what may trip teams up before they find themselves in this position.

This stage is payback time, where teams repay belief in them and deliver work and a return on expectations.

Good luck!

Understanding stakeholder needs

Before you judge a man, walk a mile in his shoes.

Mary Torrans Lathrap, 19th-century American poet, preacher and reformer

By putting themselves in their stakeholders' shoes, teams can arrive at a greater and more empathetic understanding of their needs.

What this practice can help with

Teams are set up to meet stakeholders' needs. These may not be very clear, or keep changing. A team may wish to clarify or deepen its understanding or gain a different perspective on a situation – this practice helps with that.

About this practice

This practice can help your team understand stakeholders' needs and views more deeply or differently. This can help your team take more informed decisions about its work, which is important at this stage (see Practice 7: 'Identifying key stakeholders' on page 34). This practice can be used after identifying stakeholders, to understand them more fully.

Two variants of this practice are suggested:

→ 'perceptual positions' – a technique from neuro-linguistic programming (NLP)

→ 'empty chair' or 'two-chair' – drawn from Gestalt psychology.

Both variants aim to give your team a renewed perspective on a situation. The 'perceptual positions' practice looks at a situation more broadly, from a detached view. This can be useful if there is significant emotion associated with an issue. The 'empty chair' technique can increase empathy towards a stakeholder.

Perceptual positions helps to understand others' viewpoints from three positions that a team can take:

→ first position – seeing the world through the team's eyes

→ second position – standing in a stakeholder's shoes

→ third position – neutral observer.

In this practice, a team member moves positions and perceives a situation from a range of viewpoints to arrive at different perspectives.

Time

These practices can take upwards of 30 minutes, depending on the complexity of the issue and number of stakeholders.

What you will need

Both practices require space to move around (in or outside), and sufficient chairs for each person represented. This practice can work virtually with non-speaking members' cameras turned off.

Step-by-step guide

Perceptual positions

1. A team member places a chair a few feet away from them, to represent a customer or their requirements. They stand facing this chair.
2. The other members of the team observe this practice from a distance.

3. The team member describes a current situation aloud (briefly), and *their* understanding of it. This could be about an existing or new customer request.
4. The team member moves to another position in the room and, while continuing to look at the customer, describes the same situation aloud from the *customer's* perspective.
5. The team member moves to a third position in the room, and describes the same situation aloud from a neutral, third-party perspective.
6. Invite the team to share their observations on what they have heard from all three positions. The 'issue holding' team member listens silently without responding.
7. The team member returns to their original position and shares what they have learned, including any new perspectives they have gained.
8. The team decides how to act on these new perspectives.

Empty chair or two-chair practice

1. Begin by placing two chairs a few feet apart, facing each other.
2. The other members of the team observe this practice from a distance.
3. Empty chair version: the team member sits in one of these chairs and imagines the customer or stakeholder sitting in the empty chair in front of them. They then discuss the situation with the stakeholder as if they were present.
4. Two-chair version: the team member changes positions between the two chairs and inhabits the role of the stakeholder, thinking, feeling and acting *as if* they are the stakeholder.
5. The conversation continues, with the team member as the stakeholder talking with the team member.
6. Repeat these steps until all stakeholders have been represented.
7. Invite the team to share their observations on what they have heard. The 'issue holding' team member listens silently without responding.
8. The team member returns to their original chair, and shares what they have learned with the team.
9. Debrief this as a team using these questions as prompts:
   → What would our stakeholders think, feel, say or do here?
   → What are our stakeholders' needs?
   → Are we meeting them?
   → What is most important to our stakeholders?
   → What concerns or hopes do our stakeholders have about our team?
   → What new perspectives have we gained from our stakeholders?
10. The team decides how to act on these new perspectives.

Tips on getting the most from this practice

→ Key to success here is to actively inhabit the other role. Think and act like the stakeholder.
→ Remember to de-role to avoid getting stuck in the role you have been playing. This can be done simply by moving about and changing positions.

Variations

Extra chairs can be added to understand a situation from multiple stakeholders' perspectives.

Increasing contributions in your team

Be careful what you wish for, lest it come true!

Aesop, Greek slave and storyteller

For teams to be more than the sum of their parts requires every member to pull their weight. 'Social loafing' theory suggests that a person exerts less effort to achieve a goal when they work in a group than when working alone (Ringelmann 1913). I like this quote because it sets out what every team leader wants and hopes will come true: that every member is contributing. This practice helps achieve that, helping them become more effective in the process.

What this practice can help with
Teams need everyone to play their part. Often, they don't because the leader is unaware of what the team needs from them, or the team isn't meeting the leader's expectations. This can lead to frustrations all round.

About this practice
This practice can help you or your team leader provide the leadership that the team needs, and help teams step up their contribution to make the whole team more effective.

This is an important part of stage 4, as teams focus on work and outcomes. This simple question-based practice works by anticipating others' needs. It is adapted from an activity created by American team psychologist and practitioner Bennett Bratt.

Time
→   This practice can be carried out in around 20 minutes.

→   The questions can be asked in advance to allow time to reflect on them.

What you will need
No specific materials are needed for this practice. This practice can also work just as well virtually.

Step-by-step guide
Gather the team together and ask someone (e.g. another team member or external team coach, but not the team leader) to facilitate by asking the following three questions in this order.

To the team (during which the leader should be quiet):

1.   What do you imagine team leader [name] wants more of, less of or that's different from the team to improve its effectiveness?

2.   Team leader [name] aside, what do you wish for more of, less of or that's different from the team personally to improve its effectiveness?

To the team leader (during which the team should be quiet):

3.   What do you imagine the entire team wants more of, less of, or that's different from team leader [name] to improve its effectiveness?

Open the floor to discuss and agree the actions you will take to improve team effectiveness, and meet the needs of both the leader and team better.

Tips for getting the most from this practice

→ This practice is very simple. Don't overcomplicate it.

→ The steps ask team leaders and the team to remain silent while each is being asked questions about the other. This is not a passive role: they should listen actively to the responses, both to learn from them and to understand how well the other party is aware of what is important to them. It helps increase self- and other awareness.

→ Former US Navy submarine captain, David Marquet, asked navy teams under his command: 'What am I thinking?' to encourage them to think up one level and more strategically. Operating up one level allows teams to think more widely and systemically about a situation, and anticipate issues or concerns in advance. In turn, this allows them to take early corrective or mitigating actions.

Try it yourself. It is simple – and works incredibly well.

Variations

→ Other stakeholders could be introduced into this practice (e.g. the team leader's manager, a key supplier or stakeholder group) to represent themselves and provide the team with a wider set of perspectives.

→ If it isn't possible for these additional stakeholders to be present and join the team, they can be represented in the room using an empty chair, with the team directing questions towards that (Practice 24: 'Understanding stakeholder needs' on page 80 explains how to try this).

Improving your team's routines

Your focus determines your reality.

Jedi Master Yoda, *Star Wars*

This mantra reminds us that focusing on outcomes is a great way for teams to achieve them.

What this practice can help with

Despite their best intentions, teams don't always achieve their goals: they get pulled off track but are unsure why. With hindsight, the reasons often seem familiar – at least afterwards, if not at the time. The chances are that habits or team routines are at play. A habit is acting without thinking, working on autopilot. Under pressure, we revert to habits most of the time. This is true for teams and their members.

About this practice

This practice can help your team understand what is pulling them off course. It can be used before Practice 31: 'Identifying your team's rackets' (on page 98), which explains to teams why this happens, and Practice 21: 'Identifying on-task, off-task and anti-task behaviours' (on page 70) to correct it. This Achieving stage practice helps teams focus on work and deliver outcomes, while improving their effectiveness, in two parts:

→   working out what the team's routine is

→   replacing the identified problematic routine.

The idea is to learn what triggers the team so it can choose how it responds in a situation, rather than act on autopilot and replace the current team routine with a better one. The source of this practice is unknown, although I have been using it successfully in different forms for several years with teams.

Time

→   Reflecting on an event immediately afterwards can take 1–2 minutes.

→   Doing this as a team can take longer, particularly if its routines are out of awareness and may take some spotting first.

What you will need

A diary or journal can be a useful aid to remember habitual responses. This practice can also work just as well virtually.

Step-by-step guide

Part 1: Working out a team's routine

1.   Think about occasions when your team did not achieve its outcome.
2.   What did the team do or not do that took it off track? Be specific.
3.   What were the conditions present at the time?
4.   What was the trigger that led to the team's behaviour? (This could be a comment from another team member or an agenda item, etc.)
5.   Identify the link between the trigger, routine, behaviour and outcome. You can start at either end of this sequence.

6.   Then reflect on your answer to step 5, asking yourself:

→ What purpose did this routine serve at the time it was created?

→ What benefit did this routine give the team? What was the pay-off or payback?

→ Is this routine still serving the team well?

→ What behaviour could I replace this routine with to give the team the same pay-off or payback?

→ What will tell the team this new behaviour is working?

→ What will get in the way of their sticking to this new behaviour?

Part 2: Replacing the currently ineffective team routine with a new one

Try this sequence of steps to swap the current team routine with a new and better one:

1.   Change the context – if you identify the context as the trigger from Part 1, look to change it if possible. (For example, if the team is triggered when meeting in a certain room, change the room to avoid it.)

2.   Replace the habitual team response to the trigger with a new routine.

3.   Provide the same pay-off or payback (this is the team's reward for their behaviour).

Tips to get the most from this practice

→ Routines are normal: all teams have and use them. Generally they are very useful, as they reduce the cognitive load required to execute familiar tasks, leaving teams to focus on the novel and less predictable things around them. The risk comes from their being largely unconscious, and so can be applied at inappropriate times or ways.

→ As team leader, ask yourself whether your team's routines are outdated and still serving it well.

→ Pay attention to context and content. What do you notice?

→ Working out what a routine is can be done after the team notices that it has veered off track, or by reflecting on past events.

→ Keep a diary of these events, noting the conditions at the time (best done immediately to capture the details). What patterns do you notice, e.g. does being in a team stakeholders' office trigger the routine?

→ It is easier to replace an ingrained routine with a new one, than to stop it altogether.

→ Repeating a new routine helps embed it: keep at it for change to stick.

→ Find opportunities to practice a new routine until it becomes automatic.

Variations

→ It may be easier for non-team members to notice a team's routines. Invite them to a team meeting, and ask them what they notice.

Conducting a pre-mortem to manage risks

'Mistakes... are the portals of discovery.'

From *Ulysses*, James Joyce, Irish novelist

We all make mistakes. Teams too. They can be either a source of criticism and blame or an opportunity to learn.

What this practice can help with

Projects delivered by teams are notoriously risky and frequently fail, including for reasons already known to the team. Many organisations are familiar with project debriefs that typically take place at the end of a piece of work: these focus on the past, and what went wrong. While the intention behind these de-briefs is admirable (to improve understanding), invariably they are too late to turn a project around or improve its outcomes, and little is learned from them.

There is a simple alternative: a pre-mortem. Pre-mortems anticipate and pre-empt failure, taking a future-focused stance rather than one that looks at a situation afterwards. Researchers have found that what they called 'prospective hindsight' – imagining that an event has already occurred – can increase the ability to correctly identify reasons for future outcomes by 30 per cent, says Gary Klein, Chief Scientist at Applied Research Associates in Ohio, USA.

About this practice

Most project and risk management processes rely on rational thinking, yet many of the causes of project failure are the opposite. A pre-mortem creates an opportunity to look at all possible factors without the need for hard evidence to support them since it speculates about the future.

The purpose of this practice is to show your team how to carry out a pre-mortem at the start of a new team project. This is best done after the team is clear on the scope, terms of reference and project deliverables. Through this practice, your team will anticipate what could happen in a project before it starts, and can put plans in place to prevent it from failing.

Time

Ten minutes' preparation, 60–90 minutes to carry out the practice.

What you will need

→   Flip charts and marker pens are useful for in-person teams.

→   This practice can work virtually – remote teams can use an online collaboration tool (e.g. a Trello board or Confluence page).

→   Sticky notes can be used to classify or prioritise likely risks.

Step-by-step guide

1.   The pre-mortem starts with the team leader announcing that the project has failed! Then asking the team, 'What has gone wrong with this project?'

2.   Team members write down all the reasons they can think of why the project would fail. Allow 10+ minutes for this.

3.   In turn, each member reads one item from their list of project failures until the team has a complete list of potential reasons recorded on a flip chart (or equivalent). If a prompt is needed, you could ask, 'What are the most significant risks this project faces?' Cluster the ideas into themes.

4.   Ask as a team, 'Which of the derailers we identified are most likely to happen?' Using marker pens, place dots on the riskiest potential reasons for failure identified.

5.   As a team, review the list. Ask, 'What actions do we need to take to mitigate the identified reason for failure or risk(s)?' Allocate an owner and action timeline in each case.

Tips for getting the most from this practice

→   If it's too gloomy to start with the project having already failed, an alternative is to start imagining from the present. Ask: 'What will go wrong?', or 'How might this project end as a failure?'

→   It's best for team members to note the potential reasons for a project's failure separately, so as to identify as many as possible.

→   Thinking in advance about potential project failures cues team members to look out for things that might derail them along the way.

→   Generally, smaller teams have the most open conversations. In larger groups, try using sticky notes or lists to generate ideas or split into subgroups first, before coming back together to consolidate.

→   Areas of concern and associated risks may benefit from being prioritised in terms of likelihood of occurring, and severity if they do occur – you can do this by scoring likelihood and severity out of five for each and multiplying the two figures to produce relative risk scores.

Variations

→   It can be prudent to revisit this list of potential project flaws throughout a project, and conduct periodic pre-briefs over the course of longer projects to identify new potential risks arising.

→   The team leader either can review the potential project flaws and develop a mitigation plan themselves, or do this with the team.

→   This practice works well whether in-person or virtually.

→   As well as a session asking, 'What could go wrong with this project?', a team could follow this with a session asking, 'What could go right with this project', to gather two (opposite) lists of hindering and helping factors. Both can be useful.

Learning in your team

Unless teams can learn, the organisation cannot learn.

Peter Senge, American systems scientist and Senior Lecturer,
MIT Sloan School of Management

This quotation from Peter Senge shows the role that teams play in helping organisations learn, linking them together in reciprocal roles, benefiting both.

What this practice can help with

Teams can benefit from learning from their experiences, and using this to inform new work.

About this practice

This simple practice helps teams learn from others' experiences through the medium of storytelling. This practice can help your team to improve its effectiveness, an Achievement stage goal to be reached.

American adult educator Malcolm Knowles's adult learning theory (1984) tells us that team members learn best:

→ through experience
→ when self-directed
→ when they are ready
→ through being open to learning
→ when they are motivated to learn.

A storytelling approach encompasses all these elements, and is the basis of this practice. Coach Tony Llewellyn describes a similar approach. A storytelling approach works because it:

→ engages members in the process
→ provides valuable context
→ is non-directive

– leaving it open for your team to decide the learning it will take from a story and apply.

Time

→ This practice can take 30–60 minutes.
→ Contain the time allotted to each storyteller to balance the contributions.

What you will need

Flip chart and marker pens. This practice can also work just as well virtually.

Step-by-step guide

1. Choose a topic to be discussed as an anchor for the stories.
2. Ask team members to think about an experience and be ready to talk about it openly with the team.
3. Invite one member to recount a story to the team. Allow 5 minutes. The rest of the team listens.
4. As a team, discuss the story using these questions as prompts:

    → What have we learned?

    → What do we need to change?

    → How can we embed this learning into the team's routines?

    → Do we need to update our team working agreement?

    → What new capabilities do we now have as a team?

    → How can we deploy these new capabilities?

    → What do we need to learn next?

    → How will we go about this?

    → What have we learned about how this team learns?

    → How can we adapt our approach to learning to learn quicker, etc.?

5. Ask the team to write the lessons from the story on a flip chart.
6. The team then summarises the key learning shown on the flip chart.
7. Discuss as a team how the team will apply this learning.

Tips for getting the most from this practice

→ Having psychological safety in place is important to encourage team members to take a risk as they tell stories. This can be helped by the leader going first and allowing the team to see that they do not know everything, can err and still have things to learn.

→ This practice can be used any time that a team needs to learn, or by priming teams to think about their experiences and be ready to tell a story about them.

→ Keep the focus of the story on the key elements and learning from them, rather than a blow-by-blow chronological recital.

→ The chosen story could contain positive or negative experiences, and end well or poorly. Aim for a mixture.

→ Stories that end 'happily ever after' often don't contain much learning.

Variations

Try this variation as you adapt this practice to your team and its needs. Divide the team into smaller groups to recount stories: this can make it safer to discuss less-than-positive experiences.

Playing the team joker

Let's all hail the joker. That special character...
who can break the ice, nudge the floodgates.

Alan Dymock, Scottish rugby player and *Rugby World* features editor

The role of team joker is both unusual and important. Dymock invites us to recognise and welcome the contribution it can make.

What this practice can help with

Teams have a tendency towards groupthink, which Irving Janis (1972), a research psychologist at Yale University, described as a psychological drive for consensus at any cost that squashes dissent and consideration of alternatives during decision making.

Challenging strongly-held beliefs and opinions – particularly if you are (or perceive that you are) the minority or solo dissenting voice in a team – carries inherent risks of speaking up against the majority view. Teams can benefit from finding safer, alternative ways of revealing the truth.

About this practice

The court jester has a long history in popular media over the centuries, with the joker being one of the few people who can tell often-difficult truths to those in authority. The famous diarist, Samuel Pepys (1668), explained: 'The King's fool and jester, with the power to mock and revile even the most prominent without penalty.' A modern version is that of 'devil's advocate'. The joker's role is to increase a team's self-awareness, and encourage them to look at alternatives.

This practice can help a team to remain cohesive when opinions vary, and to consider other ways of getting the job done.

Time

Awareness is often most easily created at the time something is said or done in a team. Use that moment. It can take seconds.

What you will need

→ Courage is a critical quality for the person playing the joker role.
→ A sense of humour can be useful. Use it lightly.

This practice can also work just as well virtually.

Step-by-step guide

1. The team leader starts by explaining the rationale behind the joker role, and the benefits to the team. This begins to create the conditions for this role to be successful and valued by the team.

   → Appoint a team member (or someone outside the team) as the joker.
   → The team leader could ask a member to volunteer for the role or appoint someone, or a team member could self-nominate. Irrespective, they will need sufficient permission and protection, most likely given by the team's leader, to be able to carry out the role successfully, according to transactional analyst, Pat Crossman (1966).

2. The team joker can increase team awareness by:

   → bringing in data from outside the team – e.g. stakeholder feedback

   → welcoming quieter voices – e.g. 'Who have we not heard from?', 'Whose voice is missing currently?'

3. The joker also can directly challenge and present alternative perspectives – e.g. 'I see this differently...', or 'I have another view of this...'

4. The questions the team joker might ask are endless. Some examples:

   → Are you lost in the maze? (If a team appears to be lost.)

   → Are you on or off the pitch? (If a team appears to be off-track.)

   → I hear lots of arguments. Are these reasons or excuses?

   → Is this team overcomplicating things?

   → What is tripping up this team?

5. The team joker can use metaphor to reveal different perspectives – e.g. 'If this team were a jigsaw, what pieces are not in place yet?'

Tips for getting the most from this practice

→ It may not be sufficiently safe even for a nominated team joker to reveal the truth. Creating greater psychological safety first makes this role possible (use Practice 6: 'Establishing ground rules to create psychological safety' on page 32 to help).

→ The leader has an important role here: everyone will be watching how they respond to challenge at first, and if it is welcomed, the joker will be encouraged to take more risk. It only takes one slapdown or even a lukewarm response to null the joker's effectiveness.

→ Whoever plays the team joker role, it can be easy for that person to get stuck in it, and harder still for them to shake it off. To offset this, rotate different team members into and out of this role periodically. This also helps to build more challenge capability across the team.

→ When a team member is in the joker role, it will be hard for them to play their normal role at the same time, so it can be useful to ensure their portfolio is covered in some way. This is another reason to rotate the joker.

→ Remember the Hippocratic Oath: 'Do no harm.'

→ Finally, if something feels difficult to say, it is exactly the thing that needs to be said. Speak up!

Variations

Ideally a team will develop the self-awareness, safety and learning capabilities to become its own joker and challenge itself. A person can play a joker role until such a time as the team is able to do this for itself.

Chapter 8
The Excelling stage

Don't be afraid to take a big step if one is indicated.
You can't cross a chasm in two small jumps.

David Lloyd George, British Liberal politician and former
Prime Minister of the United Kingdom

For teams to transition into the Excelling stage takes a real step up. The words of David Lloyd George urge teams to be bold enough to make this leap – even if it's a big one.

Teams that have negotiated the challenges of the Achieving stage now understand their stakeholders better, will have increased members' contributions and improved their team routines and effectiveness by learning how to learn. They will be working well and efficiently, and delivering high-quality work.

Excelling stage teams are highly effective and have been achieving outstanding results for some time. Teams will need to find ways of sustaining this success, as those that reach this level of effectiveness and performance are likely to find their work growing: they will need to think about how they can meet increased demand, including expanding their size and resources.

Team goals at the Excelling stage

To sustain their results and success, teams will need to work through and achieve the following goals:

→ find ways of sustaining current levels of performance and success
→ raise performance to even higher levels
→ recruit and integrate additional team members and resources without loss of performance.

What teams need at the Excelling stage

This fifth stage of development presents teams with the simultaneous challenges of sustaining their already impressive results while raising performance levels even higher.

The work for teams to complete at this stage includes:

→ celebrating past and recent work successes
→ optimising team task processes (Practices 26, 28 and 30 can all help with this, see pages 84, 88 and 96)
→ engaging with stakeholders about their current and future needs (Practice 24 on page 80)
→ encouraging a culture of learning, creativity and innovation to meet new and emerging stakeholder and/or customer needs (try Practices 22, 28 and 32 on pages 72, 88 and 100).

The Excelling stage practices

These practices help address these needs. It may be that innovating to improve task processes to meet current demands is enough. However, making this improvement also might entail a fundamental rethink of how the team goes about its work to meet new or latent needs, as well as raise performance standards even higher.

Good luck!

Conducting a team debrief

If you want a wise answer, ask a reasonable question.

Johann Wolfgang von Goethe, German poet, scientist and statesman

Goethe illustrates the value of questions here, and questions are at the heart of this debriefing team practice.

What this practice can help with

The best teams learn from experience. They carry out their work, reflect on it, identify key learning, make improvements to how the team works and put these into practice. But for most teams, this is far from an automatic experience.

Fortunately, a simple and evidence-based approach is at hand to help.

About this practice

The practice of debriefing arose from military wargaming in the 1970s in an approach called 'after-action reviews' (Reyes et al. 2018). Since then, significant research about how teams conduct debriefs has been carried out, with strong meta-analysis evidence confirming their benefits, including:

→ helping speed up project delivery
→ strengthening relationships
→ promoting learning
→ improving communication (see the various studies conducted by team researcher Scott Tannenbaum).

Tannenbaum also found that those teams that carried out debriefs outperformed those that didn't by more than 20 per cent.

This is the type of practice that makes the difference between an Achieving and Excelling stage team in sustaining performance. Despite this, surprisingly few teams are in the habit of conducting debriefs, and only do so when things have gone wrong. Just because something is deemed a success doesn't mean every aspect was perfect, or that there isn't an even better way to do some aspects next time. The lateness of these misses the opportunity to correct things along the way.

This practice shows team how to carry out a learning-oriented debrief.

Time

→ Debriefs can take anything from 10–60 minutes. Regular, focused ones only last a few minutes.
→ Setting the context should take 1 or 2 minutes; the debrief itself takes 5–30 minutes; any additional team leader input could take 5 minutes, and an action summary a further 5–10 minutes.
→ The frequency and timing of debriefing depend on the nature of the team's work. Many software development teams debrief daily; other teams, monthly. If you are new to debriefing, try starting weekly.

What you will need

A copy of the team's goals and objectives. This practice can work virtually, showing team's goals on screen.

Step-by-step guide

1. Allow time to conduct a debrief, giving members notice to prepare.
2. As team leader, set the context and explain why we are conducting a debrief.
3. The team leader might say: 'We want to debrief the recent project and learn from this experience. Let's discuss how we worked as a team, as well as any technical challenges.'
4. Clarify the parameters of the debrief: agree its scope, what is discussable and what is not open for debate.
5. The whole team can progress the debrief by discussing:

   → What were we trying to achieve?
   → What were our team roles, goals and priorities?
   → How clear were they?
   → What happened during the project?
   → What did we do (or not do)?
   → Where did we achieve (or miss) what we set out to achieve? (Keep this simple: 'Yes' or 'No' answers.)
   → What did we do that enabled us to achieve our goals or outcomes?
   → What went well?
   → Were there any areas where we were not entirely satisfied with how things went? Where might we look (or need) to improve?
   → How well did we work together as a team?
   → What would be the stretch that could make us even better?
   → What should we now stop, start or continue doing to help us become more effective?

6. The team leader adds any additional comments or clarifications.
7. Action planning: the team agrees clear actions and a plan to put them in place (including an owner and timeline for each aspect).
8. Follow up after an agreed period to check progress.

Tips for getting the most from this practice

→ Psychological safety is an important condition for a successful debrief, particularly if you want members to be open about things they didn't know, say or do! Leaders can set the tone for this by admitting their own shortcomings or actions first, and responding positively and without judgement to input.
→ Keep the focus on learning, rather than rehashing past events and blaming others.
→ Ask questions to find answers. Let the team identify key learnings, rather than only coming from the team leader.
→ Don't forget to balance focusing on areas for improvement with recognising what has worked well too, to reinforce successes.
→ Be inclusive, with everyone participating.
→ Give team members permission to express disappointment about setbacks. It will be hard to move forward without this.
→ Leadership consultant Doug Sundheim (2015) offers some useful insights on this topic in his Harvard Business Review article, 'Debriefing: A simple tool to help your team tackle tough problems'.

Identifying your team's rackets

Once in the racket, you're always in it.

Al Capone, American gangster and businessman

Al Capone had a different understanding of 'racket' at the time than teams do today. Nonetheless, I include it here because rackets in teams operate at an unconscious level. Unless they are made more visible, they remain out of sight, with a team replaying their racket continuously and staying 'in it'.

What this practice can help with
Our best intentions don't always lead to the outcomes we seek. The same is true for teams, and especially when their performance often dips after 18–24 months, according to Susan Wheelan, former Professor of Psychological Studies at Temple University, USA.

About this practice
As a team's remit expands in this stage and it takes on additional work, it's important to optimise its processes. This practice shows your team how to do that by explaining why teams get pulled off track. (Practice 21: 'Identifying on-task, off-task and anti-task behaviours' on page 70 can be used to spot if your team is getting drawn into unhelpful work.)

This practice follows and extends this by helping teams identify *why* this is happening. The concept of rackets is drawn from a popular school of psychology – transactional analysis – and created by Richard Erskine and Marilyn Zalcman (1979).

A racket is a familiar set of feelings and behaviours that can arise in response to a set of circumstances. These typically happen automatically and without conscious choice, which means they are not always optimised: this explains why teams can behave in ways that lead them to engage in non-essential work. It is damaging to teams, members and organisations because engaging in racket behaviours undermines team effectiveness and productivity. This practice asks a series of questions that identify the benefits and costs of your team's racket behaviours.

Time
→ This practice takes about 30 minutes.

→ Identifying rackets can be quick but can also take longer, particularly if they are entrenched behaviours.

What you will need
The whole team present for this practice, since it could be any member(s) who contributes to racket behaviour. This practice can also work just as well virtually.

Step-by-step guide
1. Start by identifying an area or topic where the team is making limited progress, or keeps getting pulled into off-task or anti-task activities.
2. Then as a team, ask:
   → What does the team intend to achieve?

→ What is this team's racket that draws us away from what we intend to achieve? (i.e. what automatic and unconscious feelings and behaviours do we need to create more awareness of that are getting in the way?)

→ What benefit or advantage does this team gain from engaging in this racket behaviour?

→ Conversely, what does it cost this team when it engages in this racket behaviour?

→ Do we want to stop this racket? If yes, what will we do as a team instead?

3. Action planning: the team agrees clear actions to stop the racket behaviours occurring, and a plan to hold each other to account for living up to these new agreements.

Tips on getting the most from this practice

→ Greater awareness of rackets gives teams the choice to act on them.

→ Be specific about the behaviours that are drawing the team away from its intention (e.g. 'We get so focused on how we might meet a new customer requirement that we forget about existing deliverables. Going forward, we will...')

→ Benefits or advantages and costs or gains can be short and longer term. Consider both.

→ Rackets can become habitual routines for teams. It can be easier to replace one routine with another, than stop an unhelpful routine altogether. Identify an unhelpful routine, then create a new one to replace it. Watch out, and say if the old one reappears. (Try Practice 25: 'Increasing contributions in your team', on page 82 to address this).

→ Rehearsal is important to embed new routines – setting up deliberate opportunities (even artificial ones) to practise can help.

Variations

→ Rather than arguing to simply stop or change a racket, the coaching questions below flip this by asking teams to consider the costs of change and benefits of not changing. This paradoxical approach can identify factors that both maintain the status quo and help unlock resistance.

→ Consider the implications of not changing. Characterise a decision not to change as exactly that – an active decision, as opposed to avoiding a decision. This paradoxical approach can identify factors maintaining the current situation and help unfreeze resistance. As a team, ask:

→ What does continuing this racket give us as a team?

→ What do we gain?

→ What are the disadvantages of changing this racket as a team?

→ What do we lose?

Getting into a creative flow

The goal of getting your team to think beyond the box is a no-brainer, but figuring out how to actually achieve greater group innovation isn't.

Rebecca Shambaugh, American leadership coach

What this practice can help with

Excelling stage teams are looking to take their performance to the next level. It may be that they're trying to improve standards, or have additional or new work assigned and need to find ways to tackle it.

How does a team raise the bar? Are its processes fit to meet these demands? Team creativity can help with these.

About this practice

These mini-practices help your team get their creative juices flowing to find alternative ways of delivering their current work or tackling additional requests. Developing new ideas creates new possibilities, but teams can get stuck in their current routines and find it difficult to think beyond this. These practices help teams to get unstuck and moving.

Time

The mini-practices below give the timings.

What you will need

The mini-practices below give the tools and resources. This practice can work virtually using an online collaboration tool.

Step-by-step guide

Getting unstuck – go see!

It can be hard to imagine a different future for the team from its usual workplace. This practice entails finding a new team base or using another location. This new environment could stimulate innovative thinking or a change of scenery could cue fresh ideas. Try it.

Apart from transport time to a different location, allow 1–2 hours for this practice.

1. Move to a new base.
2. If too time-consuming, send one or two team members on a recce to bring back ideas.
3. As a team, identify ideas generated by this new environment.
4. If it can be arranged, go and visit a different organisation facing an analogous challenge:

    → What problems are they solving? What parallels can you find?

    → What can you learn?

    → What can you offer them by way of insights?

Sketch it!

The adage, 'A picture paints a thousand words' reminds us that words can be limiting. Rather than letting them be a barrier, use hand-drawn images instead. Developing a clear and shared understanding of the problem helps find new solutions.

Provide paper and pens, and allow up to 10 minutes.

1. Sketch the problem to be solved.
2. Share your pictures with the rest of the team.
3. See what new insights emerge.

Don't worry about the quality of the sketches; this is not an art gallery!

Better questions

If you want better answers, ask better questions, says MIT's Hal Gregersen (2018b). He calls his method a 'question burst' and says that it can produce a culture of collective problem-solving when practised regularly. It sidesteps the difficulties of traditional brainstorming. This practice takes no longer than 8 minutes.

1. Describe the problem in 2 minutes or less.
2. Create the maximum number of questions possible in 4 minutes or less. The greater the number and the more challenging, the better.
3. Pick one or two questions from this list to explore further, and select one on which to act.

Developing new ideas: 'Shush!'

According to the 1960s song, 'Silence Is Golden'. It can help teams too. Brainstorming out loud tends to suit extroverted team members, and shuts down introverted ones. Try brainstorming in silence instead. Allocate 10 minutes for silent brainstorming.

1. Decide on the topic which you're trying to develop new ideas for: perhaps frame this as a question, and write it at the top of a flip chart.
2. Individually, consider and write solutions to the problem on sticky notes (one per sticky). Place them on the flip chart.
3. Then as a team, group them by theme before discussing them.
4. Discard old ideas, and keep fresher ones.
5. This can be an unusual experience for teams. Give it a go.

Tips on getting the most from this practice

Teams take the time allotted, so keep these practices short. Time pressure can be generative and avoids overthinking.

Variations

Deadlines help focus teams' efforts. Major work can be done in minutes. Working at speed and time discipline are key.

Time's up!

Try this practice out loud as a team. A clock to maintain time discipline is needed for it. Allow 15 minutes.

1. State the opportunity or problem to be worked on. Write it on a flip chart.
2. Allocate 3 minutes for the team to generate fresh ideas about it.
3. Spend 9 minutes developing these ideas further.
4. Ask the following questions and note any themes.

Preventing your team from burning out

Never give in, never, never, never, never. Never give in.

Sir Winston Churchill, former Prime Minister of the United Kingdom

'Don't give in!' is a classic organisational response to teams under pressure, and can have a positive short-term effect in encouraging them to keep persevering through challenges. However, continuing to do this over the longer term can lead to problems, including burnout.

What this practice can help with

As the chief contributor to organisational performance, teams are busy places and, with this, comes the risk of burnout. The Coronavirus pandemic has compounded this, according to a Chartered Institute of Personnel Development (CIPD) survey. This places an even greater premium on teams being able to remain resilient to continue performing.

About this practice

Other resilience practices in this book (Practices 17 and 36) focus on recovery from critical moments and setbacks. This practice shows teams how to boost their endurance resilience: when stressed from working excessive hours over a prolonged period, with a dominance of work activities.

This is a reality for Excelling stage teams, so an important practice to develop to sustain wellbeing and success. Some teams might be suffering from burnout: a state of exhaustion from too much work. This is not a mental health issue, but an organisational one – work should not make teams ill! The ultimate solution for addressing burnout rests with organisations' top leaders.

This practice shows teams ways to mitigate it by doing what they can for themselves, rather than outright prevention. Pick a practice that your team is not doing, and start to look after yourself.

Time

This practice varies from seconds to an hour.

What you will need

No specific materials are needed for this practice. This practice can also work just as well virtually.

Step-by-step guide

1.   Pay attention! We notice things we are aware of; now look out for burnout. Here are some typical cues – start with you. Ask yourself, 'Am I':

  →   feeling tired or drained most of the time
  →   feeling helpless, trapped and/or defeated
  →   feeling detached or alone
  →   having a cynical or negative outlook
  →   self-doubting
  →   procrastinating and taking longer to get things done
  →   feeling overwhelmed.

2. Are members of the team behaving differently? Are they coping? Ask team members how they are doing, giving space for a response. It takes courage to admit you aren't on top of things.

3. Don't just stand there: do something! The bystander effect is where you notice team members are struggling from burnout and don't do anything about it, assuming that others in the team have, or will. This is everyone in the team's responsibility, not just the leader's. Act now!

4. Set and hold boundaries. The best way of preventing or reducing burnout is to set and keep to boundaries between work and non-work life, according to clinical psychologist and burnout expert Michael Drayton. Ask yourself:

   → Am I okay?
   → Am I taking care of myself?
   → What are my personal boundaries?
   → Am I acting on what I'm noticing in myself and others?
   → What do I need to change to improve my exercise, sleep and diet?

5. Managing your energy is more important for high performance than managing time, advise Tony Schwartz and Catherine McCarthy of The Energy Project (2007.

6. Do this by:

   → Getting active: physical exercise is a great stress reliever and boosts energy.
   → Treat your body well: feed and water it regularly, and ensure it gets enough rest (sleep). Don't work it non-stop!
   → Notice when your energy is highest, and match your work tasks to these rhythms.
   → Improve emotional energy by appreciation and positivity. Say 'thank you' and accept others' thanks. Look for and call out positives.

7. Become more (anti)fragile. 'Antifragility' is the opposite of fragility: we get stronger when under stress, but only if we take breaks and our stress levels are not overwhelming. The Lebanese American essayist Nassim Taleb suggests we do this by:

   → building rest and recovery into our schedule
   → asking others to hold us to account for this
   → doing the same for them.

Tips for getting the most from this practice

→ Start with you: try a practice and notice the difference. Inspire team colleagues to try too.
→ 'What gets measured gets done': set one or two measures to team goals to encourage action.

Variations

Manage your mindset. There is strong evidence to support adopting a positive attitude. Try this as a team.

→ Actively look for positives.
→ Get into the habit of talking about the 'best thing at work this week'. A positive attitude is contagious. What are others catching from yours?
→ Research (Drayton 2021) shows that even a forced positive attitude can quickly become real and equally infectious (e.g. try entering a meeting with a beaming smile, and notice what you feel and see in others).
→ Try to keep things in perspective. Ask yourself, 'How important is this really? Will this matter in a week's time?'

Giving virtual gifts as acknowledgement

No act of kindness, no matter how small, is ever wasted.

Aesop, Greek slave and storyteller

'Don't underestimate the power of kindness at work,' says behavioural scientist and stand-up comedian Ovul Sezer in her 2021 *Harvard Business Review* article of the same name. The Greek slave, Aesop, would have agreed with her 2,500 years earlier. This practice is a way of showing kindness to your team colleagues.

What this practice can help with
To sustain high team performance over time, members can benefit sometimes from a bit of a boost. This can take many forms, including recognising individual members' contributions. This practice shows one way of doing this that is simple, quick and free!

About this practice
The purpose of this practice is to recognise the efforts of your team's members, so they feel that they, and their work, are appreciated. It can be used either to sustain high team performance, or to acknowledge contributions at the end of a project or team's lifespan. If the latter and a team is closing, it can create a positive ending to working in that team and help members move on to their next team successfully.

This is a simple yet effective practice that centres around the exchanging of virtual gifts between team members. It works well online, and only entails a bit of thought and no money.

Time
This practice can take 5 minutes if done individually. Add 10 minutes if working in pairs, triads or smaller groups.

What you will need
Access to the Internet to search for an image of the virtual gift. This practice can also work just as well virtually.

Step-by-step guide
Match team members together, so that each one has someone nominated to choose a gift for them (an easy way to do this is to arrange the team in a circle, and ask them to choose a gift for the person to their left).

1. The first phase involves discussion of what the ideal choice of gift would be in each case. This could be done alone by the 'gift giver', but there is more power behind the practice if it is done in pairs, triads or smaller subgroups (depending on team size).
2. The nominated gift giver leads a short discussion (2–3 minutes), and the receiver should not be present (otherwise, this spoils the gift's surprise). Once the choice is made, another giver takes the lead. It may be necessary to reconfigure the groups midway, to ensure the receivers are never party to the discussion about their own gift choice.
3. Bring the full team back together, at which point each team member in turn reveals the gift to the recipient and the rest of the team.
4. Explain the choice of gift through sharing what the smaller group discussed.
5. The person receiving the gift acknowledges it and thanks the giver.

Tips on getting the most from this practice

→ The success of this practice relies on matching the gift to the receiver, and making it something that they would really like to receive. This may mean sharing gift ideas or matching the giver to a receiver they know well.

→ The power in this practice is using the collective wisdom of the pairs, triads or smaller groups to understand the receiver well, while the receiver gets to enjoy hearing that some team members have been thinking generously about them, having put thought into their choice of gift.

Variations

This is an optional step that can be inserted between steps 1 and 2 (above). Rather than just describing the gift at step 2, if the gift giver has access to the Internet, they can search for an image of the virtual gift, and print and present (or show, if virtual) a picture of it while revealing the choice of it.

Predicting your team's future

The future is not some place we are going, but one we are creating.
The paths are not to be found but made. And the activity of making them
changes both the maker and their destination.

John Schaar, American political theorist

This quote emphasises that a team's future is not a ready-made destination, but in their own hands to invent. Working towards a new future has the potential to change this and the team itself. This is the power and potential of teams.

What this practice can help with

Teams face many uncertainties, including what lies ahead. This is particularly true for teams nearing the end of their work or lifespan, who want to know what will happen to them next. One way of predicting the future is to create it! While it might not be possible for teams to actually do this, it can be useful for them to anticipate what lies ahead, prepare to exploit opportunities and mitigate risks better.

About this practice

The aim of this practice is to help your team look ahead. It's different from the team vision and pre-mortem practices because the team has been working together for some time now and understands its context, challenges and customer needs better. These practices look both backwards and forwards. The variation at the end looks further ahead.

Time

→ 'Predicting the future from the past' takes 30 minutes.
→ The 'Bananas and bumps' practice takes 30–40 minutes.
→ Allow a few minutes to update the team on changes; longer to discuss what they mean and any actions arising.

What you will need

→ Flip charts and marker pens
→ Masking tape and sticky notes for the Bananas and Bumps practice.

This practice can work virtually using an online collaboration tool

Step-by-step guide

Predicting the future from the past

1. As a team, make a list of events that have occurred in the recent past and surprised you: e.g. budget cuts, shock resignations. Ask: 'What happened suddenly that we could have foreseen?'
2. Agree what needs to be monitored in future to reduce the chances of being caught out again: who will take ownership of this, and how it will be done.

Ask: 'What are the signs to look out for as a team that signal a change is ahead?'

3. As team leader, agree how these signs of change will be communicated to the team in future.

4. As team leader, make updating on future changes a regular fixture in your team meeting agenda.

5. Discuss how you will understand what these changes mean to the team.

Bananas and bumps

This practice can be used by a team if they're aware of challenges ahead, and need to plan for them and others that might occur, but are out of sight (called 'bananas' and 'bumps' respectively).

1. Draw a line on a flip chart or use masking tape to make a line on the floor. This line represents a timeline from now into the future (e.g. the next 12 months), and the path that the team will take into it.

2. Explain that bananas are challenges the team can see but have not yet faced and bumps are invisible but may occur.

3. Ask team members individually to note the bananas – one per sticky note.

4. List the bananas and bumps separately to create the greatest number of occurrences.

5. Place the sticky notes on the timeline at the point at which the bananas can be seen.

6. Ask team members individually to note the bumps – one per sticky note.

7. Place the sticky notes on the timeline at the point at which the bumps might occur.

8. As a team, discuss and consolidate the bananas and bumps to remove duplication.

9. Discuss mitigating actions as a team.

Tips on getting the most from this practice

Discuss mitigation actions in smaller groups if the team is large.

Variations

Leadership expert Chris Henderson (2017) suggests using visualisation to help your team look even further ahead.

1. Ask members to shut their eyes and imagine themselves at a time in the future (e.g. in 6 months). Taking your time, ask them to picture this future as if they are living it now: What do they notice in detail? What is different? How does it feel?

2. After spending time picturing the team in the future, ask the members to write down their observations. Take time here.

3. Share the images and/or observations arising across the team.

4. Ask: What stood out? What is different about the team? How did it feel?

Note any themes.

5. Ask: What is the gap between the current and future team? What actions could the team take to realise the future? What needs to be done to mitigate any risks identified?

Chapter 9
The Re-orientating stage

This is not the end or the beginning of the end but the end of the beginning.

Sir Winston Churchill, former Prime Minister of the United Kingdom

Teams at the Re-orientating stage are in between the known present and an unknown future state. Rather than a team seeing itself as closing, this quotation helps us to see that they are in a state of flux from which new possibilities will emerge.

The Re-orientating stage is a transitional stage for teams. By this stage they have been performing well for some time, and are highly effective: they will have optimised their work processes, and found new or different ways of working collectively. Individual contributions will have been recognised.

However, even high-achieving teams lose momentum over time. As identified previously, 18–24 months after forming, group effectiveness wanes and performance drops. This is normal but can come as a shock and affect the team, especially those that were previously highly performing, whose morale can dip and be tricky to pick up. Burnout can compound this.

At this point, it's time to rethink the team's purpose:

→ What work should it achieve now?
→ How should it be carried out?
→ What are the key priorities?

Alternatively, a team's work may have been completed, and the team fulfilled its purpose: it may simply have reached the end of its life cycle. Equally, a team may be unable to bounce back from a performance drop, and be closed. These last two scenarios are time for a team to prepare to end. Emotions are likely to run high and be expressed: this is normal, and attending to them is part of working through this stage.

Team goals at the Re-orientating stage

Teams will need to work through and achieve the following goals.

Recovering from a performance dip:

→ update the team's purpose, membership, roles, ways of working, processes and norms
→ revitalise the team and help it recover from declining performance
→ onboard newly-recruited members to existing team norms and processes

– or preparing the team for closure:

→ ready the team to close while completing outstanding work and sustaining performance over this time

→ help members find new roles and teams, and successfully transition into them.

What teams need at the Re-orientating stage

This final stage of development presents teams with several challenges: preparing to turn around or close, the latter with attendant emotions towards separation and loss, irrespective of why the team is closing. The work to complete varies, depending on the team's future.

Recovering from a performance dip:

→ helping the team recover from setbacks (see Practice 36 on page 112)
→ renewing the team's purpose, membership, processes and practices, as needs change (see Practices 9 and 26 on pages 38 and 84)
→ celebrating the team's efforts that have got them to this stage

Preparing the team for closure:

→ celebrating the team's successes and achievements
→ supporting team members during change and transition (see Practices 36 and 38 on pages 112 and 116)
→ acknowledging and helping members accept the closure of the team, and grieve for its loss (see Practice 40 on page 120).

The Re-orientating stage practices

This can be a challenging stage for teams as it involves significant change, whether in turning performance around or closing down a team. It can be difficult to engage members and encourage them to continue working, especially if their futures are uncertain.

This stage is important because how team members experience these changes may influence what they carry forward into their next team.

Good luck!

Helping your team recover from setbacks

It's all in the recovery.

Tavistock Consulting, UK

All teams experience the occasional setback. This quote spurs them on to thinking it is how they respond to it that counts.

What this practice can help with

Not everything goes smoothly, even for the best team. Assignments can and do hit difficulties. Teams fall behind in delivering projects, and assignments can go woefully wrong. Longstanding customers can be lost. Sought-after team projects can get cancelled unexpectedly. All these situations can affect a team's confidence adversely.

Alex Stajkovic, an organisational behaviour professor at Wisconsin School of Business, USA, reports there is strong evidence that collective team efficacy – a belief that the team will succeed in a specific task or project – is an important predictor of team performance. In other words, teams that believe they will be successful are more likely to be. However, the same is true in reverse – which is why it makes sense to boost teams' ability to recover from a setback.

About this practice

Several practices can help teams recover their mojo, including Practice 28: 'Learning in your team' (page 88), Practice 30: 'Conducting a team debrief' (page 96) and Practice 38: 'Coping with unexpected news and loss' (page 116). High individual self-belief or efficacy is not enough; what's important is that the belief that the team will succeed is shared across it.

This practice focuses on helping entire teams bounce back through different mini-practices designed to improve this efficacy.

Time

Identifying a recent experience often takes seconds. Identifying the learning can take 15–20 minutes (teams can still learn from less than positive experiences). Choosing to move on takes moments.

What you will need

No specific materials are needed for this practice. This practice can also work just as well virtually.

Step-by-step guide

Teams sometimes hold on to failure. As a team, ask yourselves:

→ Are we holding on too long to negatives and the past?

→ Is it time to let go?

→ How will we do this now?

The ELMO practice

This mini-practice helps teams do that using the acronym ELMO: Experience, Learn, Move on. Try it with your team:

1. Identify a recent shared team experience (e.g. a challenging team task that did not meet a client's expectations).
2. Reflect and learn from it. (Use the learning and debrief Practices 28 and 30 on pages 88 and 96 to help do this.)
3. Actively choose to move on from it – as a team, choose to let go of any emotional grip the setback is still having and move forward, perhaps by focusing on something new or different. A team might find a ritual to do this (e.g. screwing up a piece of paper with the setback's name on it, and throwing it into a wastepaper bin.)

Your team can invite non-team members (e.g. a member of another team or a team coach) to help facilitate your ELMO practice.

Find a quick win

Letting go of something that did not work out as we had hoped can be easier said than done – but it can be easier to do this if a negative experience is replaced by a more recent positive one.

1. As a team, identify a prospective or upcoming piece of work, project or task that is quickly and easily accomplished by everyone in the team.
2. Take it on, and complete it to the team's satisfaction. If stakeholders are happy with it too, so much the better.
3. Celebrate this success within the team.
4. Promote the success to others outside the team.
5. Identify the strengths and capabilities the team used to complete this work. Remind everyone on the team about how they went about achieving this outcome, and the part that its members played.
6. Get practising positive self-talk to bolster team efficacy.

Tips on getting the most from this practice

Think about actions the team can take to minimise (before), manage (during) and mend (afterwards) self-efficacy (belief) after a setback.

Variations

It can be easy to magnify an adverse event, and for it to become universal and pervasive across other areas of the team's work. This need not be the case, as this variation shows.

Contain it

Try to contain it to prevent it spreading.

1. Be specific about the setback situation. Be precise about the circumstances and context in which it occurred:

    → Who exactly was involved?
    → What happened?
    → When?

2. Put a boundary around it. For example, the team might draw a 12-month timeline and mark the setback on it at the time it occurred. Portraying this visually shows the team the setback as an event in the past: it should help them focus on the present and future.

Evaluating your team's effectiveness

Success can be measured by the team's own evaluation of its ability to see, name, own and work on the most important drivers of its effectiveness.

Bennett Bratt, American team consultant

What this practice can help with
While it is normal for team performance to fade over time, this can be the time to review the team's effectiveness.

About this practice
There are different ways of measuring team effectiveness, including using a diagnostic or discovery tool such as teamSalient. Alternatively, your team could evaluate itself. Irrespective of who does this, it is good practice for a team to review its effectiveness periodically. While any self-evaluation can lack criticality and objectivity, it also has some advantages: it can be done more often to improve the team continually and stem declining performance. Teams that review themselves are more likely to accept and act on the findings. This practice shows how to conduct a self-review.

Time
→ Allow 30 minutes to agree the factors to be measured.

→ Completing the evaluation can take a matter of minutes; collating the scores, longer.

→ Allow up to a further 60 minutes to agree the actions to be taken on the findings.

What you will need
Print and use a copy of Table 10 below, showing the 16 team effectiveness factors. This practice can work virtually, showing Table 10 on screen.

Step-by-step guide
1. As team leader, start by agreeing with the team why it is important to review its effectiveness, and that it will undertake this itself.
2. Decide how the evaluation will be carried out (e.g. manually or online).
3. Decide who will carry out the evaluation.
4. Carry out the evaluation. Collate the team's scores into a team profile.
5. Set a time to debrief the findings with the team, and carry this out.
6. Agree collective and individual actions, and any support needed. (Remember to appoint individuals to own actions.)
7. Put the actions into practice, then review their success.
8. Agree how often the team will review its effectiveness (e.g. quarterly), and who will do this.
9. Repeat this team effectiveness review at the agreed time.

Table 10 shows 16 factors of team effectiveness measured by the teamSalient diagnostic tool and example measurement, with sample scores in the first point of evaluation column.

Table 10: The 16 drivers of team effectiveness, measured by teamSalient

No.	Driver	Driver description	Evaluation point 1 (0–10)	Evaluation point 2 (0–10)
Fundamentals domain				
1	Leadership	How leadership is provided within the team	7	
2	Purpose	The reason the team exists and its contribution to the organisation	5	
3	Team composition	Team membership and the skills of team members	4	
4	Psychological safety	A shared belief that it is safe for team members to take risks and be themselves	4	
5	Team glue	The strength of team member interdependence and cohesion	4	
Facilitators domain				
6	Task processes	The steps a team takes to achieve its tasks	6	
7	Communications	How a team exchanges information through conversations	4	
8	Collaboration	How team members work together and with other teams	3	
9	Conflict	Disagreements between team members based on a clash of interests or beliefs	3	
10	Resources	Resources and development available to help the team carry out its work	5	
11	Learning	How the team uses and develops its members' skills and improves from feedback	3	
Fire-ups domain				
12	Achieves results	The team's results orientation and motivation to succeed	5	
13	Self-management	How team members moderate their behaviour towards each other in the interests of the team	7	
14	Courage	The strength to do the right thing for the team	3	
15	Adaptability	The ability to adapt the team's thinking and behaviour, and respond at pace	7	
16	Creativity	A culture of creating radically different ways of meeting stakeholder needs	5	
Total effectiveness score (from 160)			75/160	
Total effectiveness score (%)			47%	

Tips on getting the most from this practice

→ Agree the purpose of this evaluation from the outset (e.g. to develop, improve team effectiveness or both), and communicate this clearly to the team.

→ Agree whom the team evaluation findings will be shared with (e.g. no one outside the team, team leader's manager).

→ Decide whether the team will see its effectiveness profile before debriefing it, how this information will be shared (e.g. by email), and with whom.

→ The real value in any effectiveness review is to act on the findings.

→ Allow time between reviews for the team to improve (e.g. 3–4 months).

→ Match the frequency of the evaluation to the team's norms (e.g. biannually or quarterly performance reviews).

Variation

Alternatively, create and use your own team diagnostic such as the 'Team selfie' created by team coach trainer Allard de Jong (in Georgina Woudstra's book, *Mastering the Art of Team Coaching*).

Coping with unexpected news and loss

The most beautiful people are those who have known defeat, known suffering, known struggle, known loss, and have found their way out of the depths.

Elisabeth Kübler-Ross, Swiss American psychiatrist

Teams sometimes experience setbacks. It's how they recover from them that makes a difference. Elisabeth Kübler-Ross's words remind us that these periods are, at least for teams, generally a temporary state, and that they will emerge from them in time. Knowing this can make the challenges easier to bear.

What this practice can help with

Teams sometimes receive unforeseen news, which can throw them off track and disrupt their performance. The unexpected nature and timing of this can be as disruptive as the content of the news itself. We all go through a range of emotions on hearing something we are not prepared for, particularly if it is bad news.

For teams, this could range from a loss of critical resources, preventing them from achieving their goals to news of their premature closure.

About this practice

This practice can help your team process unexpected news and associated emotional reactions, so it can continue with its work or ready itself to close – both possible outcomes of a Re-orientating stage team. This practice draws on the work of Kübler-Ross with cancer patients and their reactions to loss, resulting in the creation of the widely and well-known 'change curve' (Figure 3).

Figure 3: The Kübler-Ross change curve

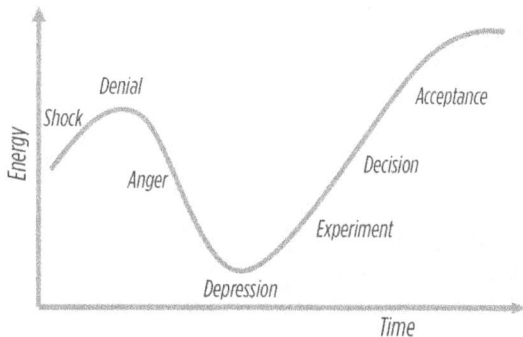

Source: Kübler-Ross (1969)

Time

Allow 30–40 minutes for this practice. Longer for larger teams.

What you will need

→ Flip chart and marker pens

→ Masking tape for floor marking (see Variations below).

This practice can work virtually using an online collaboration tool

Step-by-step guide

1. Draw the change curve on a flip chart with a marker pen.
2. Ask team members individually in turn to write their initials in a position on the curve that best shows their current emotional response to the news.
3. Assuming it is sufficiently psychologically safe, invite team members to say a little more about why they are at that place on the curve, and how they feel about it now. Acknowledge members' feelings.
4. Coaching questions to ask each other at this step include:
   → Is this news unanticipated or expected for you?
   → Are you surprised and/or shocked by it? How so?
   → How do you feel about this news? (e.g. sad, mad, fearful, angry, etc.).
   → What does this news mean to you?
   → What are the implications of it for you?
   → What does this news mean for us as a team?
5. Ask each team member what help and support they would need to move around the change curve by using the following questions:
   → What would allow you to make one step forward around the curve?
   → What support do you need to make this move and stay there?
6. Act on requests for help and support.

Tips on getting the most from this practice

→ The time it takes your team members to move through the change curve will vary. Not all of them will be at the same stage at the same time: some may progress more quickly than others, or not at all. While these differences don't make it easier to help a team move through the cycle, they are normal reactions to adverse news.

→ It can be tempting to encourage team members to move along the change curve more quickly, perhaps to catch up with others who are further ahead. This is unlikely to help, and may trigger resistance. Change takes time and so allow for this, recognising that we all grieve differently.

→ This practice may benefit from the team increasing its psychological safety to be able to engage openly within it. (Practice 13: 'Creating a team working agreement', on page 50 can help teams with this.)

→ The aim is to understand team members' emotional reactions, rather than their feeling the need to explain or justify them. Take this step before moving on to actions.

→ Encourage team members to help each other, particularly if they are at the same or similar stage on the curve – peer support will strengthen team bonds.

Variations

The change curve also can be physically mapped out on the floor (using masking tape), with team members standing at the place that shows how they feel about the news. This helps everyone see how the rest of the team feels about it, which can normalise reactions.

Practice 39
Improving your team's self-belief

To accomplish great things, we must not only act, but also dream:
not only plan but also believe.

Anatole France, French poet, journalist and novelist

Anatole France's words underline the importance of self-belief. Teams can benefit from this too.

What this practice can help with

Things don't always go smoothly for teams, even highly effective ones. They might have an unsupportive sponsor, a bout of recent poor performance or have experienced bad luck when it needed things to go right! Sometimes they experience setbacks and their self-confidence dips. We are hardwired to remember the negatives and tend to focus on failure: this can be paralysing, particularly if a team gets stuck in this mindset. This vicious cycle must be halted and reversed.

Rather than trying to stop paying attention to the disappointments, it's easier to replace them with positive success stories instead. The team's proudest moments practice (below) and Practice 26: 'Improving your team's routines' (on page 84) explain this further. The idea is to use this practice to improve the team's potency – its overall belief in its general capabilities and collective efficacy – a shared belief among the team that it can perform specific assignments well.

About this practice

The purpose of this practice is to develop your team's 'recovery' resilience. This should help them regain their self-belief when faced with adversity or things are going badly, and allow them to move on without a dip in performance in between.

This practice is drawn from the sports psychology world of elite Olympic athletes and the work of Dr Steve Bull, where high performance is rewarded with a podium place and medal. It works because it provides tangible evidence of past performance to offset negative (intangible) beliefs, and helps teams focus on learning rather than dwelling on negative outcomes.

Time

The 'team's proudest moments' practice takes 10–20 minutes.

What you will need

→ Flip charts
→ Coloured marker pens to list the proudest moments
→ Sticky tack or masking tape to visibly display the team's achievements.

This practice can work virtually using an online collaboration tool.

Step-by-step guide

The team's proudest moments

1. Invite team members to think about their proudest achievements. Ask:

    → What are we most proud of as a team?

    → What is a stand-out success?

2. Talk about them as a team. List them in order of greatest to great. Ask:

    → What did the team do/not do that led to this achievement?

    → Who else can the team tell about its achievement?

    → What have we learned from this project or task?

    → How can we use this?

3. Place the list where it is easily visible to the team to act as a reminder (if appropriate, use photographs, graphs, etc. to bring it alive).

4. Use the team's proudest moments on the list when it faces a tough challenge. Read the list regularly, to improve team-shared self-efficacy.

5. Consider what qualities the team had that were key to these successes, and whether any are relevant to the current challenge.

6. Update the list with new proud moments after fresh team achievements.

Tips on getting the most from this practice

→ Refer to Practice 26: 'Improving your team's routines' (on page 84) as a reminder on changing habits.

→ It can be important for teams to practise self-forgiveness.

→ This practice could be work-related (preferably), or non-work-related, if such moments stand out and are the source of pride for the team.

→ Your team's proudest moments could be small and still significant. Don't overlook them. Look for moments of which the whole team is proud.

→ If possible, try to match your team's proudest moments to the challenges they are facing and/or will face to make them more meaningful.

Variations

→ Instead of listing your team's proudest moments, draw them on a flip chart. This will make them more memorable for the team to recall.

→ Rather than putting the proudest moments on a flip chart, keep them in a place that's special to the team, e.g. a team room, space or box. Make them visible to act as a reminder and positive reinforcer.

Planning for your team's closure

Every exit is an entry somewhere else.

Sir Tom Stoppard, British playwright and screenwriter

This quote reminds us that as one thing comes to an end, another begins. This is true for teams at the Re-orientating stage who may be experiencing closure, but this also creates an opportunity to join a new team.

What this practice can help with

No team lasts forever. For some, their work is completed, and so the team comes to a natural end; for others, the organisation may decide to shut down and disband the team. Team members bond and form strong attachments when a team is created; these bonds are broken on disbanding, which can lead members to experience a sense of loss and grief.

How the team ends can create a lasting impression – positive or negative – and this experience can be carried forward into future teams that members join. It makes sense for all concerned to manage this ending well.

About this practice

The aim of this practice is to help your team end well, so that its members can grieve and move on to future roles successfully – a key goal for a Re-orientating stage team. As the American clinical psychologist and IMD business school professor George Kohlrieser reminds us: 'Separation can also be a positive experience at the right time and if dealt with in the right way'. This practice helps teams find the right way.

Elisabeth Kübler-Ross's (1969) well-known change/grief curve from her work with cancer patients can explain the emotional journey that team members and teams go through when experiencing loss. The context for each team will vary – including the reasons for its closure. This practice, based on one proposed by British team practitioner, Tony Llewellyn, in his book on building brilliant teams (p. 201), is best adapted to your team's particular circumstances. Speaking is central to facilitating a team's ability to handle grief, and this practice is best done together. Dialogue is at its heart.

Time

Allow 40–60 minutes for this practice.

What you will need

No specific materials are needed. This practice can also work just as well virtually.

Step-by-step guide

1. Set up a team closure meeting. Try to ensure that all team members are present.
2. The team leader begins by talking about why the team was set up and its purpose. Describe what the team has achieved. As team leader, describe your personal experience, including the ups and downs over the lifespan of the team.
3. Invite each team member to say a few words on what they appreciate about other team members.
4. Invite each team member to say what they have learned from being a member, and will take away with them.

5.   Ask the team if they would like to remain in contact, and agree a mechanism for this.

6.   Close the team by asking each member to say one or two words that provide some closure for them personally, e.g. 'I have enjoyed working with you and will miss our conversations.' Acknowledge what's important.

Tips on getting the most from this practice

→   Although the team is ending, relationships between members remain. Acknowledging this and finding a way to stay in touch can help manage the ending.

→   Team members don't need to say very much, but it's important that everyone speaks and is heard to bring about closure.

→   Try to create closure in the final statement, rather than opening things up again to support members when the team no longer exists.

→   Recognising that no team will exist forever, your team could plan how it will manage its ending before it happens to prepare members for this.

Variations

→   If a team has fulfilled its purpose and achieved its aims, the practice could be more celebratory. If a team is being closed because it has not performed to expectations, then acknowledging efforts may be the focus.

→   To ensure no one is missed out when it comes to showing appreciation, stand in a circle (or create a 'virtual table' to show where people are relative to each other, if online) and invite each person to say a few words about a quality they have noticed and appreciated in the person to their right. The response should be limited to a simple 'Thank you.' (We are very used to deflecting such words – just let them settle in and not be denied). Be careful it doesn't become a verbal CV by sticking to a single quality.

→   This can be expanded by adding an additional question about the team, such as: 'What will you miss about being on this team?', or 'What have you learned in the team that you will take forward in your future work?'

Part III
Bringing it all together

Epilogue

Making your mark on the world is hard. If it were easy, everybody would do it. But it's not. It takes patience, it takes commitment, and it comes with plenty of failure along the way. The real test is whether you choose to persevere.

Barack Obama, 44th President of the United States of America

I hope you have come to recognise that now is indeed the time for teams! Whether you started at the Orientating stage and progressed through the rest of them, or began at a later stage, I hope the definitions and six-stage model in Chapter 1 helped explain the different stages of team development and demystified the challenges to be found along the way. The first practices aimed to help you gauge whether you were ready as a team, and if the effort to develop was likely to be worthwhile. I hope it was.

If you progressed through Orientating stage 1, you will have experienced the frustrations and anxieties arising from the lack of clarity that often comes with a newly-forming team. The different practices should have helped you design and set up your team with solid foundations, and then launch it with a well-defined purpose, vision, goals, roles and set of teamworking behaviours.

By the time your team reached Resolving stage 2, you will have known the other members better, and started working together towards shared goals. The practices here will have helped your team go beyond clarifying team roles and the work to be done to learn how to handle disagreements. As a result, it should be tighter-knit and more resilient.

Compared with stage 2, the Collaborating stage should have been easier, as your team's communication and dialogue skills improved, you learned to work together and became more cohesive. If your team is effective, productive and delivering results, it has most likely reached the Achieving stage. This delivery of high-quality and quantity work would have continued into the Excelling stage, with your team achieving (and trying to sustain) outstanding results for some time.

The Re-orientating stage is a pivotal one for teams, involving either finding ways to foster higher performance, or rethinking the team's work and how it goes about it. Alternatively, your team may have reached the end of its lifespan, and be readying to close and come to terms with this.

Team development is rarely, if ever, a smooth path. If you have not progressed through these stages neatly, you are far from alone. As previously identified, it is normal for teams to get stuck in a stage for a while, or even slip backwards for a time. If you find this, it might be a signal of having skipped key activities in a stage. All is not lost: look back at the Introduction to the stage before, and check whether you have worked through the goals for that stage. If not, pick and try those practices to fill the gap: you should find that this helps you make headway again as a team.

Whatever your reason for choosing this book, I hope you have benefited from it. I'm confident that if you do the work of putting these tried-and-tested practices into action, you'll become a much more effective and higher-performing team.

Good luck!

Using teamSalient with teams

For more information on teamSalient see **www.teamsalient.com**. If you are interested in using teamSalient with teams in your organisation, do contact me at **info@teamSalient.com**.

Appendix: Resources for coaching practitioners

This section contains more detailed and/or technical information that may be of interest to team practitioners. The material is structured using the same titles as the sections in the rest of the book.

Chapter 1: The six stages of team development

What is a team?

On page 3, I define a team as:

> A collaboration between a recognised group of people drawing on individual capabilities and strengths, who are committed to working together interdependently to achieve a common purpose and collective performance and learning goals.

Let's consider these elements in more detail (Table 11).

Table 11: Elements of a team

By:	I mean:
Collaboration	The behaviour of working together
Recognised	The team itself, and others outside it, recognise who is a member of that team
Group of people	More than two people
Individual capabilities and strengths	A team is made up of individual members that brings different abilities and skills
Committed to working together	The members have agreed to this
Interdependently	Team members are reliant on each other to carry out the team's work, or achieve the team's goals
Common purpose and collective	Elements that bring the team's efforts together, so that they can be more than the sum of their parts

Chapter 2: How the practices work

What is a 'practice'?

This chapter starts by defining what is meant by the word 'practice', as this is central to this book. On page 9, I define 'practices' as:

> An approach to creating a team process founded through dialogue, improved through repetition, adaptation and reflection, and sustained by improvements to a team's overall effectiveness.

Let's explore this definition in more detail (Table 12).

Table 12: Practices defined

By:	We mean:
Creating	A creative process of discovering how to work better together as a team
Process	Team actions and collective behaviours
Improved through repetition, adaptation and reflection	A team gets better through: • reflecting together on how they have gone about a task • adapting the practice to their needs • trying the practice again • reflecting further as a team on how this new practice has worked • repeating the practice regularly.
Sustained by improvements	The practice will only become part of a team's routines if it seen as leading to recognised improvements
Team effectiveness	Wageman et al.'s (2008) definition of team effectiveness, namely that the: • team is meeting and/or exceeding its stakeholders' performance expectations • team is improving its effectiveness and capability to work together • experience of working together as a team develops members' learning and wellbeing.

What is the theory behind practices?

The practices are based on sound theoretical foundations and solid practical methods. These are summarised as:

→ appreciative enquiry (Stavros et al. 2015) – affirming strengths and successes; exploring, discovering and being open to new possibilities to find new and better ways of working
→ solution-focused approaches (de Shazer and Berg 2005) – focusing on solutions rather than problems to help a team progress
→ positive psychology – prizing and praising positives (Seligman 2011) to reinforce successes, build momentum for change and create a positive team climate
→ experiential learning (Kolb 1984) – reflecting and learning from what a team is currently doing
→ active experimentation (e.g. Schön 1991) – designing and testing new ways of working, with a focus on learning and improvement.

Glossary

Achieving	The fourth stage of team development, and the teamSalient discovery tool
Adult learning	A theory of adult learning (e.g. Knowles 1984)
Appreciative enquiry	A strengths-based, positive approach to (team) development and change
Brainstorm	An idea generation method used in teams and/or groups
Change curve	Associated with Kübler-Ross's 'stages of grief' cycle (1969)
Check-in/out	An approach used by teams at the start and/or end of meetings
Collaborating	The third stage of team development, and the teamSalient discovery tool
Collaboration	The behaviour between team members when working together
DARN	An acronym for Desire, Ability, Reason, and Need in motivational interviewing
Development stage	The different stages or levels a team moves through as it develops.
Domains	The three domains of team effectiveness measured by the teamSalient discovery tool: Fundamentals, Facilitating and Fire-ups. Each domain consists of five or six drivers
Drivers	The 16 drivers of team effectiveness measured by the teamSalient discovery tool
Excelling	The fifth stage of team development, and the teamSalient discovery tool
FSNP	Forming, Storming, Norming and Performing – Bruce Tuckman's (1965) original four stages of team development
Fundamentals drivers	The five foundational drivers of an effective team measured by the teamSalient discovery tool: they relate to structural elements of a team and can benefit from team (re-)design
Facilitators drivers	The six enabling drivers of an effective team measured by the teamSalient discovery tool: they relate to team processes and ways of working
Fire-ups drivers	The five more individual-focused drivers of an effective team measured by the teamSalient discovery tool
Gestalt	A school of psychology
Ground rules	The rules of behaviour agreed when first working in a group

HR	Human Resources
Intervention	The action or process of intervening: i.e. actions taken to improve a team
Normalise	To make normal: e.g. conflict is normalised in a team
Orientating	The first stage of team development and the teamSalient discovery tool
Positive psychology	The scientific study of positive subjective experiences that aim to improve quality of life
Practice(s)	An approach to creating a team process founded through dialogue, improved through repetition, adaptation and reflection, and sustained by improvements to a team's overall effectiveness
Practitioner	A team practitioner or coach internal or external to the organisation
Psychological safety	A shared belief that it is safe for team members to take risks and be themselves
NLP	Neuro-linguistic programming
Re-orientating	The sixth stage of team development, and the teamSalient discovery tool
Resolving	The second stage of team development, and the teamSalient discovery tool
Routine	The name for a team's unconscious habit(s)
Shift	The movement between a team's development stages
Solution-focused	A future-focused, goal-directed approach to solving problems created by de Shazer and Berg (2005)
Stages	The different stages or levels a team moves through as it develops. Popularised by the work of Bruce Tuckman
Team	A collaboration between a recognised group of people drawing on individual capabilities and strengths, who are committed to working together interdependently to achieve a common purpose and collective performance and learning goals.
Team charter	A one-page summary of team launch activities: e.g. vision, purpose, roles, goals, stakeholders, ground rules, etc.
Voting	A means of making decisions.

Further reading and resources

Alliger, G, Cerasoli, C, Tannenbaum, S and Vessey, W (2015). 'Team resilience: How teams flourish under pressure.' *Organizational Dynamics* 44: 176–184.

Aristotle (1908). *Metaphysics*, Book VIII, 1045a 8–10, trans. WD Ross, Clarendon Press.

Baldoni, J (2008). 'How trustworthy are you?' *Harvard Business Review*, 15 May.

BBC Learning English (2006) 'Learning English – moving words: Lao Tzu.' Available at: https://web.archive.org/web/20061027065217/http://www.bbc.co.uk:80/worldservice/learningenglish/movingwords/shortlist/laotzu.shtml, accessed 19 June 2022.

Bion, W (ed.) (1980). *Bion in New York and Sào Paolo*. Clunie Press.

Box, G (1976). 'Science and statistics.' *Journal of the American Statistical Association* 71(356): 791–799.

Bradley, B, Postlethwaite, B, Klotz, A, Hamdani, M and Brown, K (2012). 'Reaping the benefits of task conflict in teams: The critical role of team psychological safety climate.' *Journal of Applied Psychology* 97(1): 151–158.

Bratt, B (2020). *The team discovered: Dialogic team coaching*, BMI Publishing.

Bull, S (2006). *The game plan: Your guide to mental toughness at work,* Capstone.

Chamorro-Premuzic, T (2015). 'Why group brainstorming is a waste of time.' *Harvard Business Review*, 25 March.

Chartered Institute of Personnel and Development (CIPD) (2020). 'Embedding new ways of working post-pandemic: Employers' responses to the COVID-19 pandemic prompts renewed thinking about working practices.' September. Available at: www.cipd.co.uk/Images/embedding-new-ways-working-post-pandemic_tcm18-83907.pdf, accessed 21 June 2022.

Clutterbuck, D (2015). 'Team coaching readiness indicator', unpublished.

Costa, A and Anderson, N (2012). 'Advances and developments in trust and social capital at work.' In Costa, AC and Anderson, N (eds) *Major works: Trust and social capital in organizations*, Sage, pp. ix–xxiii.

Cross, R, Rebele, R and Grant, A (2016). 'Collaborative overload.' *Harvard Business Review*, January–February.

Crossman, P (1966). 'Permission and protection', *Transactional Analysis Bulletin* 5(19): 152–154.

de Jong, B, Dirks, K and Gillespie, N (2016). 'Trust and team performance: A meta-analysis of main effects, moderators and co-variates.' *Journal of Applied Psychology* 101(8): 1134–1150.

de Shazer, S and Berg, I (2005). *Brief coaching for lasting solutions*, W.W. Norton & Co.

Derby, E and Larsen, D (2006). *Agile retrospectives: Making good teams great.* The Pragmatic Programmers.

Dirks, K and Ferrin, D (2002). 'Trust in leadership: Meta-analytic findings and implications for research and practice.' *Journal of Applied Psychology* 87(4): 611–628.

Drayton, M (2021). *Anti-burnout: How to create a psychologically safe and high-performance organisation.* Routledge.

Duhigg, C (2016). 'Project Aristotle: What Google learned from its quest to build the perfect team', *New York Times Magazine*, 22 February. Available at: www.nytimes.com/2016/02/28/magazine/what-google-learned-from-its-quest-to-build-the-perfect-team.html, accessed 9 May 2022.

Dymock, A (2021). 'The role of the team joker in rugby.' *Rugby World*, 7 June. Available at: www.rugbyworld.com/featured/role-of-the-team-joker-in-rugby-126217, accessed 20 May 2022.

Edmondson, A (1999). 'Psychological safety and learning behaviour in work teams.' *Administrative Science Quarterly* 44(2): 350–383.

Edwards Deming, W (2022) 'The W. Edwards Deming Institute.' Available at: https://deming.org, accessed 19 June 2022.

Erickson, T (2012). 'The biggest mistake you (probably) make with teams.' *Harvard Business Review*, 5 April.

Erskine, R and Zalcman, M (1979). 'The racket system: A model for racket analysis.' *Transactional Analysis Journal* 9(1): 51–59.

Geschke, H (2010). 'Brainstorming'. In Gray, D, Brown S and Macanufo, J, *Gamestorming: A playbook for innovators, rulebreakers and changemakers*, O'Reilly Media, pp. 82–83.

Gray, D, Brown, S and Macanufo, J (2010). *Gamestorming: A playbook for innovators, rulebreakers and changemakers*, O'Reilly Media.

Gregersen, H (2018a). 'Better brainstorming.' *Harvard Business Review*, March–April.

Gregersen, H (2018b). *Questions are the answer: A breakthrough approach to your most vexing problems at work and in life*, Harper Audio.

Harrison, R (2010). 'Role negotiation: A tough-minded approach to team development.' In Coghlan D and Shani AB (eds) *Fundamentals of organization development*, Sage, pp. 55–65.

Henderson, C (2017). *Jump! Deliver astonishing results by unleashing your leadership team*, Red Door Publishing.

Hogan, R (2007). *Personality and the fate of organizations*, Lawrence Erlbaum Associates.

Ibarra, H and Hansen, M (2011). 'Are you a collaborative leader?' *Harvard Business Review*, July–August.

Isaacs, W (1999). *Dialogue: The Art of Thinking Together*, Bantam Doubleday Dell Publishing Group.

Janis, I (1972). *Victims of groupthink: A psychological study of foreign-policy decisions and fiascoes*, Houghton-Mifflin.

Kahn, W (1990). 'Psychological conditions of personal engagement and disengagement at work.' *Academy of Management Journal* 33(4): 692–724.

Katzenbach, J and Smith, D (1993). *The wisdom of teams: Creating the high-performance organization,* Harvard Business School Press.

Kierson, M (2009). *The transformational power of executive team alignment: Organizational success beyond your wildest dreams*, Advantage Media Group.

Kirkman, B, Stoverink, A, Mistry, S and Rosen, B (2019). The '4 things resilient teams do.' *Harvard Business Review*, July.

Klein, G (2007). 'Performing a project premortem.' *Harvard Business Review*, September.

Knowles, M (1984). *The adult learner: A neglected species* (3rd edn), Gulf Publishing.

Kohlrieser, G (2006). *Hostage at the table: How leaders overcome conflict, influence others and raise performance*, Jossey-Bass and Wiley.

Kolb, D (1984). *Experiential learning: Experience as the source of learning and development* (Vol. 1), Prentice-Hall.

Krylov, I (1883[1814]). 'The inquisitive man.' In *Krilof and His Fables*, ed. W Ralston, Cassell, pp. 43–44.

Kübler-Ross, E (1969). *On death and dying*, Scribner.

Leary-Joyce, J (2014). *The fertile void: Gestalt coaching at work*, AoEC Press.

Lencioni, P (2002). *The five dysfunctions of a team*, Jossey-Bass.

Levi, D (2014). *Group dynamics for teams* (4th edn), Sage Publications.

Llewellyn, T (2017). *The team coaching toolkit: 55 tools and techniques for building brilliant teams*, Practical Inspiration Publishing.

Lucas, G (1999). *Star Wars, Episode 1: The Phantom Menace*. LucasFilms.

McChrystal, S, Collins, T, Silverman, D and Fussell, C (2015). *Team of teams: New rules of engagement for a complex world*, Penguin.

Maister, D, Galford, R and Green, C (2002). *The trusted adviser*, Simon & Schuster.

Marquet, L (2012). *Turn the ship around! A true story of turning followers into leaders*, Portfolio Penguin.

Mathieu, J and Rapp, T (2009). 'Laying the foundation for successful team performance trajectories: The roles of team charters and performance strategies.' *Journal of Applied Psychology* 94(1): 90–103.

Mayer, R, Davis, J and Schoorman, D (1995). 'An integrative model of organizational trust.' *Academy of Management Review* 20(3): 709–734.

Miller, W and Rollnick, S (2002). *Motivational interviewing: Preparing people for change* (2nd edn), Guildford Press.

Obholzer, A and Roberts, V (1994). *The unconscious at work: Individual and organizational stress in the human services*, Routledge.

Pepys, S (1668). *The diary of Samuel Pepys* (Vol. 3.), Naxos.

Perry, E, Jr, Karney, D and Spencer, D (2012). 'Team establishment of self-managed work teams: A model from the field.' *Team Performance Management* 19(1–2): 87–108.

Peters, J and Carr, C (2013). *High performance team coaching: A comprehensive system for leaders and coaches*, Friesen Press.

Quinn, R and Thakor, A (2018). 'Creating a purpose-driven organization.' *Harvard Business Review*, July–August, pp. 78–85.

Reyes, D, Tannenbaum, S and Salas E (2018). 'Team development: The power of debriefing.' *SHRM Executive Network: People + Strategy Journal* 41(2). Available at: www.shrm.org/executive/resources/people-strategy-journal/Spring2018/Pages/debriefing.aspx, accessed 18 June 2022.

Ringelmann, M (1913). 'Recherches sur les moteurs animés: Travail de l'homme' [Research on animate sources of power: The work of man]. *Annales de l'Institut National Agronomique* 12(2nd series): 1–40.

Schaar, J (1981). *Legitimacy in the Modern State*. Transaction Publishers.

Schön, D (1991). *The reflective practitioner: How professionals think in action*, Ashgate.

Schwartz, T and McCarthy, C (2007). 'Manage your energy, not your time.' *Harvard Business Review*, October.

Schwarz, R (2002). '8 ground rules for great meetings.' Roger Schwarz & Associates. Available at: www.schwarzassociates.com/8-ground-rules-for-great-meetings, accessed 23 December 2021.

Seligman, M (2011). *Flourishing: A new understanding of happiness and wellbeing*, Nicholas Brealey.

Senge, P (1990). *The fifth discipline: The art and practice of the learning organization*, Random House.

Sezer, S, Nault, K and Klein, N (2021). 'Don't underestimate the power of kindness at work.' *Harvard Business Review*, 7 May.

Shakespeare, W (2015[1603]). *Hamlet*, Act III, Scene I, Penguin Classics.

Shambaugh, R (2019). 'How to unlock your team's creativity.' *Harvard Business Review*, 31 January.

Sharma, V, Roychowdhury, I and Verma, M (2009). *Why do wilfully designed teams fail? Factors leading to team dysfunction*, Icfai University Press.

Simons, T, McLean Parks, J and Tomlinson, E (2018). 'The benefits of walking your talk: Aggregate effects of behavioural integrity on guest satisfaction, turnover, and hotel profitability'. *Cornell Hospitality Quarterly* 59: 257-274.

Spencer, D (2010). 'The anti-problem, games for opening.' In Gray, D, Brown, S and Macanufo, J, *Gamestorming: A playbook for innovators, rulebreakers and changemakers*, O'Reilly Media, pp. 80–81.

Stajkovic, A, Lee, D and Nyberg, A (2009). 'Collective efficacy, group potency and group performance: Meta-analyses of their relationships and test of a mediation model.' *Journal of Applied Psychology* 94(3): 814–828.

Stavros, J, Godwin, L and Cooperrider, D (2015). 'Appreciative Inquiry: Organization development and the strengths revolution.' In Rothwell, W, Sullivan, R and Stavros, J (eds) *Practising organization development: A guide to leading change and transformation* (4th edn), Wiley.

Sundheim, D (2015). 'Debriefing: A simple tool to help your team tackle tough problems.' *Harvard Business Review*, 2 July.

Taleb, N (2012). *Antifragile: Things that gain from disorder,* Random House.

Tannenbaum, S and Cerasoli, C (2013). 'Do team and individual debriefs enhance performance? A meta-analysis.' *Human factors* 55(1): 231–245.

Tannenbaum, S and Salas, E (2021). *Teams that work: The seven drivers of team effectiveness,* Oxford University Press.

Tannenbaum, S, Beard, R and Cerasoli, C (2013). 'Conducting team debriefings that work: Lessons from research and practice.' In Salas E, Tannenbaum S, Cohen, D and Latham G (eds) *Developing and enhancing teamwork in organizations: Evidence-based best practices and guidelines*, John Wiley & Sons, pp. 488–519.

Tavistock Consulting Service (TCS) (2020). 'Advanced Coaching Practice Online', unpublished course notes, 14 July.

Tolle, E. (2001). *The power of now: A guide to spiritual enlightenment*, Yellow Kite.

Torrans Lathrap, M (1895). *Judge softly: Rare gems from the literary works of Mary T. Lathrap,* Woman's Christian Temperance Union.

Tuckman, B (1965). 'Developmental sequence in small-groups.' *Psychological Bulletin* 63(6): 384–399.

Tuckman, B and Jensen, M (1977). 'Stages of small-group development revisited.' *Group and Organization Management* 2(4): 419-427.

Wageman, R (2019). 'What are the 6 conditions?' *6 Conditions certification*, unpublished.

Wageman, R, Nunes, D, Burruss, J and Hackman, J (2008). *Senior leadership teams: What it takes to make them great*, Harvard Business School Press.

Webster, D (2021). *Creating adaptable teams: From the psychology of coaching to the practice of leaders*, Open University Press and McGraw-Hill.

West, M and Markiewicz, L (2016). 'Effective team working in health care.' In Ferlie E, Montgomery, K and Pedersen A (eds) *The Oxford Handbook of Health Care Management*, Oxford University Press, pp. 231–252.

Wheelan, S (2013). Creating effective teams: A guide for members and leaders (4th edn), Sage Publications.

Woudstra, G (2021). *Mastering the art of team coaching*, Team Coaching Studio Press.

Yerkes, R and Dodson, J (1908). 'The relation of strength of stimulus to rapidity of habit-formation.' *Journal of Comparative Neurology and Psychology* (November): 459–482.

Acknowledgements

Many people contribute to a team's work, and the same is true for this book.

First, let me thank the dozens of teams I have worked in and with over the years. These experiences provided the impetus for this book and, to support them, encouraged me to write it. Many of the practices contained in this book have either arisen from work with these teams, or because of it. I hope you have benefited from them.

I would like to acknowledge Georgina Woudstra, founder of Team Coaching Studio, with whom I discussed early ideas for this book. (You can read more about her innovative work training team coaches in her 2021 book, *Mastering the Art of Team Coaching.*)

I want to offer my thanks to Carroll Macey and Emily Jones, who added to two of the practices, and give particular thanks and appreciation to Andy Fryer, who proofread the entire book and made many improvements. All three are excellent teamGenie team coaches.

I would like to remember my great friend of more than 30 years, Andy Croft, who passed away before this book went into print but who, nonetheless, thought it was a 'super, excellent idea'. I hope you find the reality matches this.

About the author

Dr. Declan Woods is a top team psychologist, who specialises in working with boards and leadership teams, and Professor of Leadership Practice at King's College London.

Declan leads teamGenie®, an international company specialising in designing, coaching and developing teams (www.teamgenie.com), and is on a mission to help teams release their magic. When this happens, teams triumph. After receiving numerous requests for help from teams, Declan wrote this book to show teams how to triumph themselves.

Declan was the first Master Coach accredited with the Association for Coaching (AC) and is a Chartered and Registered Psychologist. He led the creation of the AC's executive and team coaching standards and accreditation schemes, and co-authored and launched the Global Code of Ethics (www.globalcodeofethics.org) signed by the world's leading coaching bodies. He was made a Lifetime Fellow by the AC for raising standards of coaching globally.

Declan writes a regular column on team coaching topics and is a frequent commentator on teams in the press. He created the award-winning diagnostic tool teamSalient® (www.teamsalient.com) to help organisations drive improvements in team effectiveness.

EU Safety Representative: euComply OÜ Pärnu mnt 139b-14 11317 Tallinn
Estonia hello@eucompliancepartner.com +33 756 90241

www.ingramcontent.com/pod-product-compliance
Lightning Source LLC
Chambersburg PA
CBHW081506200326
41518CB00015B/2398